When
Students
Choose
Content

**CORWIN
PRESS**

The Corwin Press logo—a raven striding across an open book—represents the happy union of courage and learning. We are a professional-level publisher of books and journals for K–12 educators, and we are committed to creating and providing resources that embody these qualities. Corwin's motto is "Success for All Learners."

When Students Choose Content

A Guide to Increasing Motivation, Autonomy, and Achievement

Jeff Passe

CORWIN PRESS, INC.
A Sage Publications Company
Thousand Oaks, California

For information address:

Corwin Press, Inc.
A Sage Publications Company
2455 Teller Road
Thousand Oaks, California 91320
e-mail: order@corwin.sagepub.com

SAGE Publications Ltd.
6 Bonhill Street
London EC2A 4PU
United Kingdom

SAGE Publications India Pvt. Ltd.
M-32 Market
Greater Kailash I
New Delhi 110 048 India

Printed in the United States of America

Library of Congress Cataloging-in-Publication Data

Passe, Jeff.
    When students choose content : a guide to increasing motivation, autonomy, and achievement / Jeff Passe.
        p.   cm.
    Includes bibliographical references and index.
    ISBN 0-8039-6448-X (alk. paper). — ISBN 0-8039-6449-8 (pbk. : alk. paper)
        1. Student participation in curriculum planning—United States.
    2. Classroom management—United States. 3. Motivation in education—United States.   I. Title.
    LB2806.15.P383   1996
    371.1'023—dc20   96-18455

This book is printed on acid-free paper.

96 97 98 99 00 10 9 8 7 6 5 4 3 2 1

Corwin Press Production Editor: S. Marlene Head

Contents

Administrators and Parents • Step 9: Planning the Initial
Lessons • Step 10: Planning the Rest of the Unit • Step 11:
Managing the Unit • Step 12: Concluding the Unit • Step 13:
Reflect, Revise, and Publicize

Preface

In recent years, schools have been moving away from centralized decision making. Inservice training, for example, is increasingly becoming a school-based issue, rather than a districtwide one. The same is true for such matters as teacher hiring, equipment purchasing, and disciplinary structures.

In the spirit of decentralization, school principals are likewise passing on decision-making power to grade-level teams and to individual teachers. This trend has come about, in part, because superintendents and principals have such overwhelming responsibilities that they cannot handle them all. But it is also a function of teacher empowerment. After all, it is argued, teachers are trained to be professionals and should therefore be given more responsibility.

Amid this movement, it is to be expected that decisions about curriculum would also be affected. Choosing the content that is taught and learned is, perhaps, the most important set of decisions that educators face.

The case for decentralized curricular decision making has several strong arguments. First is the belief that students have differing needs that cannot be met by a single broad curriculum. Second is the idea that educational leaders have a better understanding of their students than some central authority in the state capital or county seat. Third is the growing recognition, based on a strong research base, that teachers already make several important curricular decisions throughout the school day.

Curricular decision making comes in a variety of models. Of particular interest to many teachers is the model that includes students in the process. Although originally based on Rousseau's Romanticism, the theory was developed and popularized by Dewey. It has appeared in various incarnations, including Dewey's University of Chicago Laboratory School and so-called "free schools" of the 1960s and 1970s. The most recent research and philosophy concerning constructivism, emancipatory interest, brain research, and quality schools have all lent support for this model. As the decentralization movement concurrently picks up steam, the idea of student input into the curriculum will continue to increase in popularity.

This book will explore the concept of student curricular decision making. It will present the theory and research behind the movement, procedures for creating the model, and descriptions of the model in practice. Teachers and administrators who read this book will be able to make adaptations to their own classrooms and schools to allow students a role in the curriculum decision making process. If done successfully, we can help to create a world where students become the motivated, autonomous, lifelong learners and citizens needed to sustain democratic societies.

Creating a classroom in which students choose the content may seem impossible to teachers who struggle to cover all of the content that is required by their states and districts. That concern is legitimate, and it is addressed in this book along with other concerns such as student behavior management and administrative support. Teacher concerns are a central focus of this book, because unless educators believe in the process, the movement for student curricular decision making will never grow.

I feel confident in advocating this approach because I have tried it myself. I taught two one-period classes in a local middle school during the fall semesters of 1990-1991 and 1991-1992 in which the students chose the content. Many of the tips that are offered come from my own experiences, particularly my mistakes.

The first year's class is extensively described in Chapter 4. During the second year, I used what I had learned from the first experience. The success of the second course convinced me that the process does indeed work. It also reminded me that as students and circumstances change, curricular adaptations will constantly need to be made. This book must, therefore, only serve as a handbook, rather than a foolproof guide, because the unexpected is bound to occur. Such a warning will not be upsetting to most teachers, for they recognize that classrooms are dynamic places where teachers must be flexible. If that were not the case, why would we need teachers at all? The computers would have taken over long ago!

This book would never have happened without the significant efforts of several outstanding educators. Stephanie Counts, Tom Spivey, and the entire faculty of Piedmont Open Middle School in Charlotte demonstrated true professionalism when they let a college professor come to their school to try out his radical ideas. Kathy Willox and Steve Hunt are both marvelous teachers who inspired and encouraged me on a daily basis. I learned so much from them about middle school, teaching, and life. Two administrators at the University of North Carolina at Charlotte, Corey Lock and Bill Heller, granted me course release to allow this experiment to occur. Their commitment to partnerships between universities and public schools should not go unrecognized. Maria Yon played a major role in the entire project by visiting my classroom, collecting and analyzing research data, and constantly pushing me to reflect upon and record my thoughts and experiences. My wife, Mindy Passe, was and is a wonderfully creative educator with a zeal for excellence. Any success I achieve is, in some way, related to her as well as my children, Sarah and Ryan. Finally, my fondest appreciation goes to my middle school students: Jason, Bianca, Emre, Rashonda, Shane, Bianca, Hassa, Misty, Reggie, Katie, Gray, and Ryan in Year 1; and Dara, Julie, Curtis, Chris, Brian, Taryn, Chad B., Chad M., Dondre, Jake, Trish, Corey, Angela, and Jermaine in Year 2. We learned and we had fun—a great combination!

JEFF PASSE
University of North Carolina
College of Education
Charlotte, NC 28223
jpasse@unccvm.uncc.edu
January, 1996

About the Author

Jeff Passe has taught courses in curriculum and social studies at the University of North Carolina at Charlotte since 1986. He taught in elementary and middle schools before earning a doctorate in Curriculum and Instruction from the University of Florida. From 1990 to 1992, in addition to his university responsibilities, he returned to the classroom to teach two semester-long middle school courses on current issues. He has published articles in more than two dozen professional journals and has written three elementary-level textbooks and a college text, *Elementary School Curriculum*. Passe currently serves on the Board of Directors of the National Council for the Social Studies.

1

Why Involve Students in Choosing Topics of Study?

High School Social Studies

Last week, at East High School, a popular student was suspended for plagiarism. The next day, students in Mr. Daniel Ryan's class wanted to talk about the issue of cheating. It was on everyone's minds.

"What about cheating would you like to discuss?" Mr. Ryan asked.

The noise level rose as the students conferred. Finally, Mr. Ryan called for quiet. Gradually, hands began to be raised.

"What exactly is plagiarism?" Several heads nodded in approval of that question.

"Who made this stupid law, anyhow?" An indignant murmur followed.

"Can you really be arrested for copying from the encyclopedia?" Nervous laughter and sheepish grins filled the room at that point.

"Politicians cheat. Business owners cheat. Doesn't everyone cheat sometimes?" Now the students were excited.

"Nobody gets hurt. What's the big deal?"

Mr. Ryan was overwhelmed. These were very good questions. He was forced to limit the students' input for a moment so all the topics could be recorded on the chalkboard. As he did so the students continued to suggest additional topics to each other.

There was a time when Mr. Ryan would have called a halt to the entire episode. He was a social studies teacher. The students' questions were unrelated to his units on American history and government. But he had learned something from his first experiences with student curricular decision making: *Most topics can be related to the standard course of study.*

Take these questions on cheating. They could be used to introduce the Constitution, Congress, and the judicial system. He could bring in the idea of copyrights and the economics of publishing. The class could discuss the impact of copyrights on foreign trade, and bring in NAFTA (North American Free Trade Agreement), GATT (General Agreement on Tariffs and Trade), and other trade pacts. The students could examine famous events of dishonesty in government and industry, such as Watergate, Tammany Hall, and the robber barons.

This unit could be a lot of fun. It would be stimulating and motivating. Best of all, in one unit he could meet many of the state objectives that he was required to teach.

High School Art

As an art teacher, Mrs. Kitty Pepper rarely worried about meeting state and district objectives or preparing students for end-of-the-year tests. Compared to the other teachers in her high school, she had relative freedom in choosing content. Therefore, when her principal suggested a student-centered program, her only concern was whether it could work for the art curriculum.

Would the students' content decisions be sufficiently art related? Would they allow her to teach the skills and concepts that she had always included in her courses? Would the topics they choose require additional time and energy, two resources that were in limited supply?

Mrs. Pepper was pleasantly surprised to discover that her students made a series of wise choices. But she was not so sure at first. When she was given their choice of topics, she saw that the consensus was to begin by studying the art that appeared on inserts in their compact discs. This was a far cry from her standard September unit on the Impressionists. Would class time be wasted on such trivia as rock stars' photographs?

After giving it some thought, Mrs. Pepper began to see some potential, recalling her own fascination with album covers back in the days of vinyl records. She recalled a few that even used classical paintings as cover art. A study of cover art could address style, theme, and the interplay between graphic and nongraphic art. The students could expand their traditional concept of art by including photography, collage, and clothing design in their studies.

As she examined her own CD collection, Mrs. Pepper discovered another aspect of art, one that is often overlooked—mechanical design. The CD boxes were ingeniously engineered to be light, compact, and inexpensive while they protected the disc from dust. Double-disc boxes used a hinge to create access to two discs in the same box. Sometimes the disc itself had a photo or drawing printed on the plastic. Mrs. Pepper planned to have the students use their study of CD design to recognize how need influences creativity and how technology has influenced art history.

The more she thought about it, the more excited she became. The students' topic choice was ripe with possibilities. Yes, she thought, it will be more work on my part. Planning will take longer. But she was already spending an inordinate amount of time trying to motivate the students to look at art as anything but a frill. With this unit, she could spend her time on other issues. Motivation was assured. After all, it was the students' own choice of topics.

Middle School Mathematics

When he first became a math teacher, Mr. Richard Shulman relied on the textbook for his curriculum. It was orderly and efficient, just like the problems in the back of the book. Besides, that was the way he had been taught, and he grew up loving mathematics.

Mr. Shulman therefore was surprised when his professional organization, the National Council of Teachers of Mathematics (NCTM), came out in favor of connecting mathematics with other school subjects. He was immediately skeptical. How could he prepare his students for the end-of-year tests if he also had to teach social studies, science, and reading? He did not know how to teach those subjects— he was a math teacher. He was intrigued by the idea, but he could not imagine implementing it.

Later that year, Mr. Shulman was approached by Ms. Rubin, who was a science teacher and grade-level chair. In conjunction with the school theme of "Saving the Environment," her students wanted to do an environmental field study on the effects of composting leftover cafeteria food. They could perform the experiments in science class, but Ms. Rubin lacked the time and expertise to conduct the data analysis. The school principal had suggested that Mr. Shulman do it as part of the math class.

Faced with such powerful pressure, Mr. Shulman reluctantly agreed to integrate the science projects with his own curriculum. His reluctance melted away, however, when he sat down to plan with Ms. Rubin. He was pleasantly surprised to discover several mathematical applications in the students' project. To make it even better, the applications incorporated content that was required in the 7th- and 8th-grade curricular guides. Figure 1.1 shows the connections Mr. Shulman identified.

Mr. Shulman noticed several positive changes during the composting activity. These students seemed to be much more interested in the mathematical applications than they were in the textbook problems. They worked hard to solve the problems, particularly when they were faced with the challenge of building three identical compost boxes.

Mr. Shulman also found teaching more enjoyable with this project. Of course, it is always more pleasurable when students are motivated. But he also enjoyed using concrete examples instead of the fictional situations presented in the textbook. Students asked more questions this way, and test scores were higher too. What made him happiest, however, was that his students never once asked, "Why do we have to learn this stuff?"—even with algebra and geometry. He concluded that the National Council of Teachers of Mathematics had the right idea after all.

Middle School Special Education

As a middle school special-education teacher, Ms. Sarah Allison has always had to face problems with the curriculum. Because her students tended to be weak readers, the grade-level textbooks were usually unsuitable. The children were bored, frustrated, and unmotivated.

Ms. Allison wanted materials that would interest thirteen-year-olds, but the only "high interest–low reading level" books were about sports, pets, and dating. Her classes enjoyed them, but they did not fit the district's curriculum guidelines for middle school.

Usually, Ms. Allison just ignored the district requirements and worked on developing reading skills. Doing so often provoked feelings

Scientific Procedures	7th- and 8th-Grade Mathematical Applications
Step 1: Measuring how much garbage is currently produced by the cafeteria operations	Estimation Using fractions and decimals Standard algebraic order of operations Determining degree of accuracy Converting measurements
Step 2: Building compost boxes outside the cafeteria by developing a blueprint, creating a model, and building three identical structures	Using fractions and decimals Lines and planes Relationship between linear dimensions and perimeter, area, and volume Pythagorean theorem Relating second- and third-dimensional geometric figures Symmetry, similarity, and congruence
Step 3: Measuring the amount of garbage produced after composting	Estimation Using fractions and decimals Standard algebraic order of operations Determining degree of accuracy Converting measurements
Step 4: Comparing "before" and "after" measurements	Comparing phenomena Estimation Using fractions and decimals Standard algebraic order of operations Arithmetic sequences Proportion and percent

Figure 1.1. 7th- and 8th-Grade Mathematical Applications in an Environmental Project[1]

1. Project: The effects of composting leftover cafeteria food.

Scientific Procedures	7th- and 8th-Grade Mathematical Applications
Step 5: Determining how much landfill space is saved by the composting project	Using fractions and decimals Standard algebraic order of operations Developing formulas Converting measurements
Step 6: Calculating the financial benefits of composting	Money Converting measurements Estimation

Figure 1.1. Continued

of guilt because her students were missing out on valuable content, especially in social studies and science. The students would be lost if and when they were mainstreamed into regular classes.

When Ms. Allison heard about student curricular decision making, she was inspired by its dominant theme: Instead of using books to promote student interest in learning, she could let their interests determine what books should be read. If her students could choose the content, she thought, they would want to read. The motivation would come not from threats of low grades, or the possibility of rewards, but from the intrinsic satisfaction that comes from learning something you want to know.

For example, if her class decided to learn more about cars, she would gather magazines, manuals, and other materials that would answer their questions. They would develop their reading skills, but also learn science—automotive science—the physics of combustion engines and the chemistry of motor oil. There would be social studies too, as they explored motor vehicle laws, the history of automobile production, and its major economic impact on our society. They could develop mathematical skills by calculating engine performance, creating graphs to interpret findings, and examining industry statistics. This would not be boring textbook math, but real problem solving concerning questions for which the students sought answers. The arts, music, physical education—it was all there.

Ms. Allison was exhilarated to recognize this key to unlocking her motivation problem. But she was sobered by the challenge. It would change her role considerably. She would no longer be a paper pusher, shrugging her shoulders at the children's complaints of irrelevance. She now had to be a facilitator, gathering learning resources based on the children's requests. At first the thought was daunting, but then it grew in appeal. She would get to use her teaching skills. And her students would finally learn. It would be worth it.

First Grade

When Greenway Elementary School moved to an integrated curriculum, Mrs. Betty Smith, a first-grade teacher, began to let her students choose the content. At first, she was hesitant, worried that important content would not be covered.

That concern quickly dissipated after she introduced the theme of "Homes." When asked what it was about homes they wished to study, the children brainstormed a variety of questions, including:

- Why do people move?
- How do they decide where to build houses?
- How do animals choose their homes?
- Why are some houses built so closely together?
- Why do some people live in apartment buildings?
- What happens to people who lose their homes in a fire?
- Why do houses cost so much?

As the teacher reviewed the list of questions, she was struck by the range of school subjects that were addressed. In the first question, "Why do people move?" there was opportunity to incorporate each of the school subjects. Figure 1.2 outlines those connections.

By carefully examining the other questions, Mrs. Smith discovered that most of her grade-level objectives would be addressed by this initial unit. Her students would learn the skills of reading, writing, and arithmetic, but the learning would take place in the context of learning about homes.

Previously, Mrs. Smith had taught a unit on homes as part of the standard first-grade social studies curriculum. Her lessons on animals

Class	Focus/Assignment
Literature	Reading *I'm Moving* by M. W. Hickman
Language Arts	Interviewing people who have moved; reporting on their reasons
Mathematics	Tabulating the reasons for moving; presenting the findings using bar graphs
Social Studies	Marriage, divorce, leaving home upon adulthood, job changes, and death as reasons for moving
Health	How allergenic plant life is a factor in people's comfort
Science	How habitat influences plant life; how location on Earth influences temperature and humidity
Arts	Examining and creating artwork related to people moving

Figure 1.2. Integrated First-Grade Curriculum Based on the Question, "Why Do People Move?"

and graphs had also been done separately. The same was true for her skill instruction in reading and writing. Now, the students' questions gave her a system for organizing her integrated unit.

The Curriculum Belongs to the Students

Every teacher faces a unique set of challenges. Students are so different from year to year, day to day, subject to subject, even hour to hour, that planning is often an exercise in taking risks and working with uncertainties.

Will the students be motivated by your new unit? We all know that last year's success may be this year's failure.

How could an activity go so well one period and be a disaster the next? The personalities of students, the time of day, and (according to many teachers) the weather have a lot to do with it.

Usually, the reaction to content will differ from student to student in the same class. We often teach to half the class, struggling to reach the rest. A handful of students are sometimes deemed unreachable. Some teachers, when confronted with these dilemmas, shrug their shoulders. The curriculum, as they see it, is beyond their control. It is determined by the state, by the district, by the end-of-year tests, or by the textbooks. All they have to do is instruct. If the curriculum is inappropriate or boring or irrelevant, there is nothing they can do.

It does not have to be that way. Teachers can and do make curricular decisions, whether they realize it or not. They choose to emphasize certain topics, hurry through others, or maybe even skip a portion of the official curriculum. Many will introduce their hobbies or interests, such as quilting, skiing, or the Renaissance, even if it is not a designated topic in the curriculum guide. They do not do it to be "subversive," necessarily, but because those decisions are best for the children they teach. They are exercising their professional responsibilities.

Parents and administrators do not object when teachers' curricular decisions are responsible ones. Only the foolish or harmful decisions are likely to lead to negative consequences. Indeed, the best teachers we know are the ones who adjust the curriculum to meet their students' needs.

These exemplary teachers have earned their reputations because their students are motivated to learn. They not only lead the horses to water, they put salt in their oats to make them drink! But not every teacher has the gift of making outstanding curricular decisions. And sometimes even the most astute teachers will make mistakes.

The possibility of making poor curricular decisions is reduced when students are given the responsibility of choosing content. Students tend to select topics that interest them, thus avoiding motivation problems. Their choices reflect their actual needs, rather than those perceived by adults. It makes for a more efficient curriculum development process.

Curricular decision-making power belongs in the hands of students because it is their lives that are being affected—their day-to-day school lives and also their future lives. Giving them this power is not a fad, or a way for teachers to pass the buck. It is a method of developing autonomy, motivating children to learn, and developing strong citizenship skills. In this book, you will learn how to help students make the kind of curricular decisions they need to develop as autonomous, lifelong learners.

2

How Educational Theory and Research Support the Model

What We Can Learn From History and Theory

Does the following statement ring true?

The public schools, both higher and lower, were (and still predominantly are) places where accumulated knowledge about the world of nature and its processes was retailed by the middle-man, the teacher, to the learner, who received, memorized, and, without assimilation, regurgitated such facts. These facts were (and are) selected with little reference to their actual incorporation in the child's world of experience. Such a selection completely divorced the intellectual content of knowledge from the active experience of the child, robbed it of value to him, and made a bore of learning. (Dewey, 1936)

This analysis of the educational experience was written in 1936, lamenting a lack of progress over the previous 40 years. A century has passed from the time American philosopher John Dewey first argued that the curriculum must be child centered—that is, geared toward student needs and interests. During this period, scholars and educators have discussed, interpreted, and often misinterpreted Dewey's ideas. Unfortunately, in the view of many educational critics, the above statement still holds true.

Dewey's Child-Centered Curriculum

Dewey's emphasis on a curriculum relevant to children's interests has led to a series of misinterpretations that have distracted from, and even perverted, his message. Taba (1962) called it "among the most misunderstood issues of education" (p. 284). Contrary to some educators' beliefs, Dewey rejected the Romantic view that children should have *total control* of the curriculum, which he characterized as "a free flow of experience and acts which are immediately and sensationally appealing, but which lead to nothing in particular" (Dewey, 1936, p, 469). His argument was that children's interests should be taken directly into account in constructing a course of study (Kliebard, 1986).

Dewey created his own Laboratory School around the turn of the century to develop and test his idea of a student-centered curriculum. The school's curriculum was determined in advance, based on the teachers' expectations concerning students' interests. In an attempt to link the home and school lives of the child, primary-level classes studied sewing, cooking, and carpentry, with a gradual move, in the later grades, toward studies of industry and invention (Dewey, 1936). In this fashion, students' interests were taken into account.

If Dewey's approach appears to be less than radical, one must consider the historical context. The early public school student spent the vast majority of the day memorizing textbook passages in order to recite them for the teacher when called upon to do so (Tanner & Tanner, 1975). A curriculum based on students' interests was, indeed, an extreme change.

Historical Developments

In the 1960s and 1970s, Dewey's concept of child-centered education evolved into so-called "free schools," many of which relied on the Summerhillian philosophy of allowing students to study whatever and whenever they wanted. It was against this extreme that Dewey's followers protested. They argued that giving students total control of the curriculum negated the role of the teacher and discouraged serious inquiry.

The negative public reaction to this extreme version of student curricular decision making forced the pendulum to swing in the opposite direction. Instead of modifying the weaknesses of the movement, political and educational leaders implemented what they called "back to basics." This orientation, with its mandated standards, testing practices, and teacher-centered instruction, halted most of the experiments in student curricular decision making.

Recent studies indicate that student involvement in curriculum decision making has been minuscule. Goodlad (1984) reported that two thirds of students say they have no voice in curricular matters. Two surveys addressing the same issue found no input at all from students (Kingston & Anderson, 1982; Phillips & Hawthorne, 1978). In a critique of schooling practices, Ripley (1984) characterized the lack of opportunities for student autonomy as miseducative.

Contemporary Constraints

In this day of mandated curricular guidelines, there is little opportunity even for teacher input, so student curricular choices are extremely limited. The influence of textbooks, standardized tests, and overworked teachers contribute to this phenomenon (McNeil, 1986). Apple (1983) and others have railed against "teacher-proof" curriculum that de-skills teachers by taking them out of the curriculum development process. Faced with a loss of curricular input, Apple (1982) suggests, teachers will then put forth more effort to control students, thus further restricting freedom.

Concerns about students' abilities to make responsible choices may explain their lack of input into the process (Kohn, 1993). Goodlad and Su (1992) identify three immediate constraints on student curricular decision making:

1. The possibility of failing to comply with state requirements
2. The inconsistency of student preferences
3. The argument that it "is unreasonable to expect students to show an interest in something they know nothing about, and so the very learning most needed to broaden their perspectives goes by the board because they expressed no interest in it" (p. 336)

In their review, Goodlad and Su (1992) lament the lack of large-scale, long-term studies on this form of curriculum development. Indeed, the research review for this book found a series of anecdotal reports with little analysis, either quantitative or qualitative. I have addressed the question of whether these constraints will prevent the success of a student curricular decision making model with my own experiment, which is described in Chapter 4.

Benefits of Including Students in Curricular Decisions

Involving students in curricular decision making improves the following areas of student performance:

- Autonomy
- Student learning
- Motivation
- Classroom behavior

Autonomy

Dewey sees autonomy as a major ethical responsibility of the school, one that will give the student "such possession of himself that he may take charge of himself; may not only adapt himself to the changes which are going on, but have power to shape those changes" (Dewey, 1964a, p. 114). In an earlier work, he predicted that by "providing [the child] with the instruments of effective self-direction, we shall have the deepest and best guarantee of a larger society which is worthy, lovely, and harmonious" (Dewey, 1899, p. 40).

The need to develop autonomous individuals was also cited by Piaget (1932), who differentiated between autonomous, or self-directed, individuals and heteronomous, or other-directed, individuals. The latter were described as conforming, egocentric, rigid, and dependent, holding a blind faith in authority. Developing and maintaining a dynamic democratic society, one of the major goals of the educational system, requires a citizenry with more characteristics of autonomy and fewer of heteronomy.

Do we want a society in which citizens merely do as they are told, in which they never contribute to or question the decisions that our leaders make? That is a recipe for a dictatorship. Throughout history, the common people have rallied against tyranny, seeking to empower themselves. In the United States, that battle initially was fought in the 18th century, but additional skirmishes continue to this day. Around the world, new democracies are just beginning to experience the rights and responsibilities of democratic citizenship.

Gaining the right to political autonomy has been, and continues to be, a difficult task for most of the world's peoples. Carrying out citizenship responsibilities may be less traumatic, but it too is a challenge. Citizens are not born with the ability to manage their affairs, whether on a societal or individual level. Citizenship knowledge and skills must be learned. Although families, churches, and community organizations are valuable in developing autonomous citizens, schools also can play a major role in the process.

The goal of autonomy, however, is not easily addressed by a school system in which subject matter that consumes the vast majority of the school day is chosen without student input. The official process of curricular decision making places that power in the hands of adult political figures and educators.

Student Learning

Students often describe school content as irrelevant and boring (Goodlad, 1984). The content may be interesting or valuable to academics, teachers, and the general public, but the learner is the prime audience. Subject matter that the child views as irrelevant

> causes the child and the curriculum to be set against each other. . . . The subject matter . . . has no direct relationship to the child's present experience. It stands outside of it. . . . The material is not translated into life-terms, but is directly offered as a substitute for, or an external annex to, the child's present life. . . . It remains an idle curiosity, to fret and obstruct the mind, a dead weight to burden it. (Dewey, 1964b, pp. 352-353)

In other words, such content is unlikely to be learned. In a well-meaning attempt to transfer important knowledge to students, we educators sometimes present knowledge for knowledge's sake. The students do not appreciate it, apply it, or retain it. School becomes a place of absurdity, in which children perform tasks not because they are useful in the present or the future, but because they have been required to do so by some higher authority.

Depth is another consideration. Dewey (1964b) pointed out that subject matter that does not come from the students' interests becomes shallow.

> Those things that are most significant to the scientific man, and most valuable in the logic of actual inquiry and classification, drop out. The really thought-provoking character is obscured, and the organizing function disappears. Or, as we commonly say, the child's reasoning powers, the faculty of abstraction and generalization, are not adequately developed. (p. 354)

In other words, children do not learn to think under these circumstances.

Motivation

Student motivation, which is a constant concern of teachers, is a related issue. According to Dewey (1964b), "There are not only no facts or truths which have been previously felt as such with which to appropriate the new, but there is no craving, no need, no demand" (p. 353).

Faced with students who do not seek to learn the subject matter, teachers are forced to rely on motivational techniques or reward systems to get students to learn the material. Such attempts remove the intrinsic reward that comes from learning. It is no wonder that students are slow to gain an appreciation for school knowledge and skills. On the other hand, if the content has "an appropriate place within the expanding consciousness of the child, if it grows into application in further achievements and receptivities, then no device or trick of method has to be resorted to in order to elicit 'interest'" (Dewey, 1964b, p. 355).

DECI'S FINDINGS ON MOTIVATION

Recent research on motivation tends to support Dewey's thesis. Deci (1992) reviewed dozens of studies related to factors that enhance intrinsic motivation and interest, including several that focused on public school classrooms. He concluded that "social contexts that allow the satisfaction of three basic needs (autonomy, competence, and relatedness) will promote intrinsic motivation" (p. 56). It is the role of the teacher or parent, he suggests, to "take account of the person's dispositions and the available affordances, so as to create an optimal person-activity match" (Deci, 1992, p. 61). When teachers do provide for autonomy, competence, and relatedness, "optimal educational outcomes" result (Deci, 1992).

Student involvement in curricular decision making can create the social contexts that Deci (1992) recommends for increased intrinsic motivation and, ultimately, optimal educational outcomes. The first context, autonomy, is, of course, the basic goal of the process. The entire process is designed to develop a sense of autonomy in the students we teach.

A sense of competence, the second context, will promote motivation only when it is self-determined. The student must have a sense of personal causation for whatever outcome was achieved. (Fisher, 1978). Thus, when students have input into educational activities that turn out to be successful, the resulting sense of competence will promote intrinsic motivation. However, when students have little say in the decision-making process, even a successful activity will not promote a sense of competence.

The third context, relatedness, is established through genuine interpersonal involvement. When students negotiate curriculum choices with each other and their teachers, they interact over matters with tremendous relevance to their daily lives. The decisions they make determine whether what they do in school will be of interest and importance. They will, therefore, put energy into their interpersonal relationships in order to make decisions that will please each other. Out of this mutual satisfaction comes relatedness.

In classrooms and schools that do not have student curricular decision making, there is little opportunity to develop a sense of relatedness during academic activities. Important discussions and decisions take place on the playground, in after-school activities such as clubs and organizations, or on the trip to and from school. Those are times when an adult is not making decisions for the children. Feelings of relatedness must be brought into the academic classroom. Otherwise, according to Deci's studies, students will not be intrinsically motivated by school activities.

Classroom Behavior

Teachers spend far too much time attending to student misbehavior. Goodlad (1984) has estimated that 40% of classroom time is devoted to behavior control. Although that percentage must vary considerably among teachers, anyone concerned with quality education recognizes the need to minimize misbehavior.

To solve a problem, we must first define it. Misbehavior, in this case, refers to the most common frustrations teachers have in trying to promote learning: unnecessary talking, failure to follow directions, incomplete assignments, and other off-task behavior. It does not include such serious matters as fighting, stealing, and drug abuse, although, as you will see, these problems are often outgrowths of the more common misbehaviors.

The next step in solving a problem is to analyze its causes. Why do students misbehave? Educational critics cite several explanations for student misbehavior, including poor parental modeling, excessive television, peer pressure, and even genetics. All of these possible causes, however, cannot be directly addressed by schools.

BORING TASKS

There is one cause of student misbehavior that schools can address—the boring, trivial nature of school tasks (Doyle, 1986). Children spend thousands of valuable school hours completing exercises that offer no intrinsic satisfaction. They may, for instance, be copying sentences from the chalkboard, correcting textbook passages that lack capital letters, or completing a series of quadratic equations. Children learn at an early age that some of these "busywork" activities have no value outside the classroom. The only reason to participate, therefore, is to receive a good grade or avoid punishment.

Many teachers assign busywork activities as a management device. Even though the activities may have some educational value in terms of practicing skills, they are often used to keep students occupied while the teacher tends to other instructional chores. The sameness of these exercises may be appealing to some students because they tend to reduce the high level of anxiety that accompanies more challenging tasks. Unfortunately, when time is spent on such low-level activities, there is insufficient opportunity to prepare students for the more demanding expectations of the school's curriculum (Doyle,

1986). The students may, for instance, be able to color a map of Africa but may not be able to analyze current events in that continent.

The irony of using busywork as a management device is that such activities promote misbehavior. Students are most likely to hold unnecessary conversations or stare out the window when they are not interested in the task at hand. But when students have chosen the content, boredom is minimized. School activities will be started and finished with enthusiasm only when the students look forward to learning whatever the activities have to offer them.

Think about the chores you had when you were growing up. You probably hated having to wash dishes or mow lawns. Boredom comes when we are obligated to perform tasks that we do not wish to do. We usually completed the tasks at the very minimal level of performance. As adults, we may still dislike those same chores, but we do them, and do them well, because they serve a purpose. Dishes are washed because cleanliness is essential to health. We mow because we want the lawn to look good. We are motivated to work hard when the end result is meaningful and useful. Otherwise, like our students, we misbehave.

Somewhere along the way, we have learned the value of preliminary tasks. The self-discipline that comes from that lesson is best learned when we are responsible for our decisions. Lazy dishwashers grasp the consequences of dirty dishes when ants have infested the kitchen. Whoever was supposed to mow the lawn recognizes why neighbors are sending dirty looks across the hedges. By the same token, students who do sloppy schoolwork may need to learn the long-term consequences—not just low grades or missed recess, but lack of knowledge and skill for subsequent school tasks. The tendency toward misbehavior is reduced when students choose to learn preliminary knowledge and skills (such as multiplication facts or the key elements of the Bill of Rights) because they recognize their value.

Now, take this train of thought one step further. Sometimes we perform tasks with relish. We take pleasure in decorating the house for the holidays or planning an exciting lesson that we look forward to teaching. The same is true for learning. Why else would anyone choose to take adult education courses in gardening, home repair, or stamp collecting? Learning is entertaining when the lessons are of value. There is no misbehavior in these classes. The following story, taken from my own experience, illustrates what I mean.

One evening, when I was a fourth-grade teacher, I received what I thought was an irate phone call from a parent.

"What have you been doing with those kids?" asked Rodger's mother.

I tried to imagine what I had done wrong. "I'm not sure what you mean," was my hesitant response.

"Rodger went down to the basement to do some school project at 2:15 this afternoon and he won't even come up for dinner. I have never seen him so excited about an assignment! What are you having them do?"

It really was nothing special. Instead of assigning topics for the unit on research skills, I let them choose their own. Rodger had chosen the history of baseball. He must have been enjoying it. Isn't that what education is supposed to be about?

Teachers are continually concerned about time. They are often forced to hurry through the content, settling for only shallow coverage. Ultimately, important segments of the curriculum go untaught. Drama, science experiments, debates, and other meaningful learning experiences may be sacrificed because of schedule considerations. Now, imagine what could happen if the 40% of classroom time that is spent on behavior management were substantially reduced. Such a saving in time can be achieved when students are intrinsically motivated to learn. The comfort and security of a well-behaved classroom is an additional bonus for student and teacher alike.

Links to Current Educational Trends

Brain Research

The brain is the primary organ involved in learning. Educators have always sought to understand its inner workings in order to maximize student achievement. Fortunately, in recent years, developments in medicine and computer technology have permitted researchers new perspectives on the ways that the brain processes information.

Although brain research reports are quite technical and often confusing, the key findings may seem remarkably familiar. Indeed, most of the brain research has served to confirm certain aspects of educational theory (Caine & Caine, 1991). The findings that are relevant to

---

- Multiple complex experiences are essential for meaningful learning and teaching.

- Multiple concrete experiences are essential for meaningful learning.

- The search for novelty and challenge is a basic function of the brain.

- The brain tries to create patterns.

Figure 2.1. Brain Research Findings Relevant to Education

student curricular decision making are listed in Figure 2.1 and discussed below.

- *Multiple complex experiences are essential for meaningful learning and teaching.* The brain is capable of making connections from a variety of perspectives at one time. Immersion in a topic is, therefore, the best way to learn (Caine & Caine, 1991). As you will see in the following section, research indicates that students do not learn well under the traditional approach of discrete learning modules. When students make curricular decisions, they are likely to choose broad, complex topics rather than specific skills or subtopics, thus maximizing learning. Their experiences will enable them to see "the big picture," which promotes long-term memory.

- *Multiple concrete experiences are essential for meaningful learning.* Brain activation is highest when content is connected to some aspect of the students' lives. The material must be relevant (Caine & Caine, 1991). When students make curricular decisions, they will choose only topics that evolve out of their own experiences, thus maximizing attention and, ultimately, learning.

- *The search for novelty and challenge is a basic function of the brain.* Not only is the brain comfortable with novelty, it actually seeks it out. There is an endless search for meaning (Caine & Caine, 1991). Novel stimuli and challenges are constantly available in classrooms in which students make curricular decisions—both from the decision-making process itself and the interesting content that is chosen.

- *The brain tries to create patterns.* When the brain is confronted with the novel, complex data that it seeks, it tries to organize that information. This process creates meaning and promotes long-term memory (Caine & Caine, 1991). Thus only when the curriculum is meaningful, such as when students actually choose the content, will the brain be used in an optimum way. Content that is not selected by the students is less likely create patterns in the students' brains.

Progressive educators are excited about these brain research findings because the results endorse much of their philosophy. We are still learning about the functions of the brain and the ways that educators can be more effective in using brain research. In the meantime, student curricular decision making is one of the approaches, along with whole language reading, integrated curricula, and others, in which brain research may be effectively applied.

Teaching in High-Poverty Classrooms

Along with classroom behavior management and managing time constraints, the education of children who come from low-income families is frequently considered the foremost challenge of our school systems. Despite teachers' best efforts, their students tend to be unable to overcome such poverty-related problems as family instability, economic hardships, poor nutrition, inadequate housing, and unhealthy lifestyles. These problems are compounded if students who have a low socioeconomic status (SES) also have difficulty grasping the English language and North American customs (Knapp, 1995).

Most, if not all, of these problems have their roots outside the school building. Teachers can do little, by themselves, to solve them. A societal effort is required, one that will demand substantial resources of energy, creativity, and money. In the meantime, teachers must deal with high-poverty classrooms and schools as a fact of life in today's world. As societal solutions to poverty are debated, something must be done to meet the educational needs of low-SES students.

Fortunately, a growing body of research has been developed to explore this issue. Researchers have identified two approaches to education in high-poverty classrooms that significantly differ in their effectiveness. The first is called "conventional wisdom."

In brief, the conventional wisdom focuses on what children lack (e.g., print awareness, grasp of Standard English syntax, a supportive home environment) and seeks to remedy these deficiencies by teaching discrete skills (e.g., decoding skills, language mechanics, arithmetic computation). Curriculum and instruction follow a fixed sequence from "basic" to "advanced" skills, so that students master simpler tasks as a prerequisite for the more complex activities of comprehension, composition, and reasoning. To inculcate these skills, the conventional wisdom favors a style of teaching in which instruction is fast-paced and tightly controlled by the teacher to maximize student time on task. (Knapp, 1995, p. 6)

The problem with the conventional-wisdom approach is that it is effective only for certain types of outcomes and only for a short period of time. Research on its effects reveals that low-SES students will show a short-term gain on standardized tests, but will steadily fall behind their classmates after 2 or 3 years. The improvement in standardized test scores is only temporary because the tests present the same type of discrete skill exercises as the conventional-wisdom instructional methods (Means & Knapp, 1991). The students' level of understanding is not measured by these tests. Although a rise in test scores is often greeted with public enthusiasm, many educators have long recognized that those results do not necessarily translate into present or future success. The true goal is student-motivated learning that is sustained over time.

Alternatives to the conventional wisdom approach are called "teaching for meaning." Each of these alternatives

de-emphasizes the teaching of discrete skills in isolation from the context in which these skills are applied. Each rests on the assumption that knowledge is less discrete, less separable into distinct subject and skill areas. Each fosters connections between academic learning and the world from which children come. And each views the children's cumulative experience of that world as a resource for learning. (Knapp, 1995, p. 7)

A curriculum that emphasizes teaching for meaning can be developed when students are given the power to make curricular choices. Consider the three curricular principles suggested by advocates of this approach that are presented in Figure 2.2.

- Make connections with students' out-of-school experience and culture.
- Embed instruction on basic skills in the context of more global tasks.
- Focus on complex, meaningful problems. (Means & Knapp, 1991, p. 8)

Figure 2.2. Principles Guiding Instruction of Low-SES Students

Notice how student curricular decision making can promote these three principles:

1. *Make connections with students' out-of-school experience and culture.* When adults make curricular decisions, there is a possibility that the learning will not be connected to the children's experience base. However, when children choose content, they make their choices solely from their experiences.
2. *Embed instruction on basic skills in the context of more global tasks.* When students decide what to study, every skill they learn will be in context. Reading skills are acquired when the answers to their questions are in written form. They learn to write a business letter when they have to send away for information. Map skills are developed when the information on a map offers information they need.
3. *Focus on complex, meaningful problems.* Cognitively demanding tasks can be provided by a program in which students choose content because the curriculum is flexible. Instead of a textbook or curriculum guide determining which tasks will be emphasized, it is the students and their teachers who have control over schoolwork. Simple tasks are performed as a matter of course; no instruction is necessary. But as students seek greater depth of understanding, they will constantly be challenged by more demanding tasks. It is the traditional adult-centered curriculum that places unnecessarily low ceilings on student task acquisition.

This exciting body of research challenges the conventional wisdom that has stifled the growth of students in high-poverty classrooms.

Giving low-SES students the power to choose content may facilitate their successful passage through school and life.

Constructivism

The principles that have been advocated for students in high-poverty classrooms come from the resurgent philosophy of constructivism. The constructivist learning model evolves out of the student-centered theories of Dewey (1913), Piaget (1929), and Vygotsky (1962).

> It focuses more on students than teachers. With the emphasis on the learner, we see that learning is an active process occurring within and influenced by the learner as much as by the instructor and the school. From this perspective, learning outcomes do not depend on what the teacher presents. Rather, they are an interactive result of what information is encountered and how the student processes it based on perceived notions and existing personal knowledge. (Yager, 1991, p. 53)

Constructivism differs from objectivism, its opposite, in its views of knowledge and reality. Objectivists believe that reality exists separately from the individual who confronts it. From the constructivist perspective, "Reality does not exist separately from the observer, 'out there,' needing only to be discovered. There are many forms of reality, each depending on the observer's frame of reference and interaction with the observed" (Shapiro, 1994, p. 7). Objectivists believe that knowledge is neutral, whereas constructivists believe that it is constructed (thus the title of the model).

The student curricular decision-making model capitalizes on constructivist principles in several ways. When students begin to take control of their own learning, they also gain the power to construct meaning. They start the learning process from their own perspectives instead of someone else's. Instead of relying on teachers or books for their versions of reality, students are figuring things out for themselves. The process is active, rather than passive. Meanwhile, the teacher's role changes from knowledge bearer to that of facilitator.

The constructivist approach is increasing in popularity, challenging the dominant objectivist view, with alternative curricular models in most curricular areas, such as the whole language approach to reading (Britton, 1972). Constructivism appears to be motivating teachers to change their approaches to classroom instruction, but they are still choosing content for the students. By granting that power to students, they can take a further step toward true constructivist principles.

Quality Schools

Total Quality Management is a movement based on W. Edwards Deming's approach to business management. Using his experiences with Japanese industry as a model, Deming described ways to revolutionize the workplace. William Glasser applied Deming's principles to the field of education. Glasser's *The Quality School* (1990) outlines six conditions of quality schoolwork, two of which are relevant to student curricular decision making.

Glasser's first condition is a "warm, supportive atmosphere." He argues that teachers and students should avoid the adversarial relationship that plagues nonquality programs. Frequently, this relationship is caused by teachers forcing students to learn material that does not interest them.

An adversarial relationship is prevented, in part, by Glasser's second condition, that students be asked to do only useful work. Busywork would, therefore, be banned from a quality school. So would memorization, unless the students saw the benefit of memorizing the information. When students recognize, for instance, that memorizing arithmetic facts will make their calculations more efficient and accurate, they will take the trouble to do so.

Glasser describes several strategies for creating a quality school curriculum that would meet these two, as well as the other four, conditions. The key to his approach is creating a school in which students want to work hard and learn. Student curricular decision making can meet these conditions because coercion and busywork are unnecessary when students are making their own curricular choices. When all content decisions are the students' own choices, the teacher does not have to coerce. Any work the students do is done willingly to achieve a learning goal that they themselves have set. It has to be useful.

Glasser's ideas go beyond curricular decision making to address other vital issues, such as grading, staffing, and maintaining the physical plant. His quality school model could easily incorporate student curricular decision making.

Emancipatory Interest

In recent years, the topic of student curricular decision making returned to the forefront when several critical theorists critiqued the role of the curriculum in maintaining an unjust social order. Access to curricular decision making was an important concern. Apple (1982), for instance, discussed how schools alienate students by restricting opportunities for them to formulate their own aims and goals.

Much of the discussion regarding critical theory is based on Habermas's concept of emancipatory interest. The emancipatory interest, which Habermas views as the human orientation toward freedom, is linked with autonomy and responsibility (Grundy, 1986). The skills of autonomy and responsibility, his followers argue, must be developed within the structure of the school if they are to be used outside of it. Therefore, students must be included in the decision-making process, the most important of which may be the process of choosing topics of study.

With respect to the issue of how much power students should have, a popular solution is the "negotiated curriculum" (Boomer, 1982). A negotiated curriculum avoids both extremes—total teacher (or state) control, on the one hand, and total student control of the topics to be studied, on the other—thus allowing for the benefits of both, while avoiding their dangers. As Shor (1992) puts it, "education for empowerment is not something done by teachers to students for their own good, but is something students codevelop for themselves, led by a critical and democratic teacher" (p. 20).

In a review of experiments in which students and teachers negotiated the curriculum, Grundy (1986) concluded that "students were emancipated from dependence upon the teacher's ability to diagnose appropriate learning experiences. By reflecting upon their own individual and collaborative processes of learning, students were better placed to take control of the construction of their learning" (p. 123).

3

A Step-by-Step Guide to Promoting Student Curricular Decision Making

Overview

Planning a program based on student curricular decision making seems like a contradiction. If the students make all the decisions, why does the teacher have to do any planning?

In actuality, planning a student-centered curriculum requires more effort and skill than traditional programs. There is no textbook to slavishly follow, nor a curriculum guide to go by. Teachers have to consult resources, plan learning activities, acquire materials, and design evaluation components without knowing, for certain, what will be taught, when it will be taught, or even *if* it will be taught.

If that sounds daunting, rest assured that it is easier than it sounds. You may recall the fright that accompanied your first teaching assignment. You probably had to deal with unfamiliar textbooks, students whose names you thought you would never learn, and routines for every occasion, from completing attendance forms to referring unruly students to the office. All that paled in comparison to the overwhelming task of conducting lessons dealing with subjects about which you were barely knowledgeable while you maintained classroom order. Somehow, you managed to pull it off, or else you probably would not be reading this book.

Student curricular decision making requires different types of planning skills. Although it may be more difficult, it is also more rewarding because, unlike with traditional planning, teachers get the maximum use of their talents and skills to promote lifelong learning. It is not for everyone, however. As you read this chapter, plus the rest of this book, you will get a better idea of whether this is the right approach for you. The true test, of course, is to put it into practice a time or two. The 13 steps in the planning process are listed in Figure 3.1.

Step 1: Getting Permission

Talk to supervisory administrators about your plans for student curricular decision making. Doing so is more than just a professional courtesy; it is essential to the success of the program.

Administrators are ultimately responsible for what goes on in the classroom. As one principal friend of mine facetiously explains, "That's why we get the big bucks." Whatever your beliefs about the salaries or qualifications of school administrators, the level of their support can make or break the experiment.

Advantages of Consulting Administrators

Talking to an administrator before you start provides a series of benefits. The administrator may

- Identify potential obstacles in your plan
- Refer you to colleagues who may wish to work with you
- Suggest resources that may be helpful
- Serve as a buffer between you and potential critics
- Shepherd the plan through higher levels of administration, if necessary
- Recommend trying the plan as a pilot project for one unit
- Offer good advice regarding particular instructional strategies
- If nothing else, force you to develop your ideas in a presentable form

This last benefit is often the most crucial, because the plans you prepare will guide you through the process. As we all know, what may seem like a good idea in our heads can appear positively silly

Step 1: Getting permission

Step 2: Creating the optimum conditions

Step 3: Brainstorming topics

Step 4: Pruning the list

Step 5: Reaching a consensus

Step 6: Identifying subthemes

Step 7: Determining the sequence of subthemes

Step 8: Communicating with administrators and parents

Step 9: Planning the initial lessons

Step 10: Planning the rest of the unit

Step 11: Managing the unit

Step 12: Concluding the unit

Step 13: Reflect, revise, and publicize

Figure 3.1. The Planning Process, Step by Step

when it is articulated for the first time. But the more we talk or write about it, the easier it is to identify and correct weaknesses in the proposal. The trick is to do all that fine-tuning before presenting the proposal to administrators.

The Proposal (Plan A)

Your proposal should be clear and thoughtful. Be specific in identifying which of the school's goals will be met by your program and how maintaining a teacher-based or textbook-based curriculum may deter the school from meeting its goals. Your district probably has documents that refer to development of student autonomy and citizenship skills, for example. Use them to make your case.

Provide persuasive rationales for student curricular decision making. The rationales should be grounded in theory and research to avoid seeming like the latest fad. Chapter 2 of this book will be helpful in compiling this section of the proposal.

Finally, offer a step-by-step plan for implementing student curricular decision making. Use specific examples from your grade level and subject area(s) to demonstrate that you have considered the matter carefully. Specific plans for evaluating the success of the program should be included too.

Political conditions in your school or district may not support radical changes. If that is the case, propose a limited version of the model. Offer to try it for a single unit or subject area as a trial run. That gives all parties the opportunity to assess the effectiveness of the approach at the end of the experiment. If administrators find the plan persuasive, you will be ready to move to the next step.

Plan B

Of course, it is possible that your proposal will be denied. At that point, you have several options:

- Shrug your shoulders and store the plan in your "Maybe Someday" file.
- Allow the initial proposal to sink in for a while, then review it again in a few weeks.
- Ask for specific feedback on how to improve the plan.
- Revise the proposal to run over a shorter time period or with a smaller portion of the class.
- Develop support for the idea from colleagues, parents, students, and other administrators.
- Implement the plan without permission.
- Get into a screaming match with the administrator.
- Transfer to a school or school system that would be likely to allow curricular experimentation.

The best option for you depends on your reading of the school's political situation. Obviously, there can be severe consequences for some of these options. Get advice from respected colleagues before you act. But keep in mind that maintaining the status quo may have negative consequences too. Doing nothing can stifle your professional development, leave you frustrated about not meeting student needs, and result in your exit from the profession.

Step 2: Creating the Optimum Conditions

In all likelihood, your students have rarely been asked to make decisions of any kind, especially curricular decisions. Unless they are very young, they will probably be surprised, suspicious, cautious, and maybe a little bewildered. Under those circumstances, it is best to ease them into the process.

Briefing the Students

Begin by describing what the students should expect. Let them know that they will be choosing the topics to study during a particular period of time. It may be for a semester or for the entire year. At the very least, the student-controlled unit should last at least a few weeks. Otherwise, the unit will end before the experiment has been properly conducted, and neither you nor the students will get to experience the pleasures that come from student autonomy.

Clarify that your traditional role will be changing and that you will no longer decide which topics to study or rely on the textbook for those decisions. Instead, explain that the teacher will serve as a facilitator, collecting materials and planning lessons based on the students' preferences. This change may be unsettling for some students, but reassure them that learning will not be sacrificed.

At this point, a discussion of rationales is in order. Identify the potential benefits of student curricular decision making, both for the individual and for society. Of course, those benefits should be explained in concrete terms. Don't, for example, discuss "motivation." Instead, tell the students how interesting schoolwork will be when they decide what to study. Use several appealing examples of topics, underscoring the fact that you are only citing possibilities.

Ground Rules

At this point the students will be, at the very least, intrigued. A few may wish to begin right away. An initial experience in student curricular decision making may be tempting, but the class is not yet ready. A set of ground rules must be established first.

In sports, ground rules are designed to maximize fairness. Baseball's ground rules, for example, clarify for the umpires how the rules will be applied to the specific playing field. The rules tell the coaches what will happen if a ball rolls under the fence or if a designated hitter can be used. These clarifications ensure that both teams are aware of the rules, thus avoiding arguments during the heat of competition.

In student curricular decision making, ground rules meet a similar purpose. They clarify the rules for choosing topics and prevent hard feelings later on. Because students are not accustomed to voicing their opinions or having their decisions actually count, they need new ground rules to govern their behavior.

Different classes tend to have different ground rules because circumstances change from room to room. Elementary-level ground rules will differ from the middle school's, an integrated class will have different needs from those of a departmentalized language arts class, and so on. Indeed, as part of the democratic system, students in each classroom should be encouraged to help design their own ground rules.

Despite variations from class to class, the following basic principles (see also Figure 3.2) are recommended in designing a set of ground rules:

- *Students get to choose their topics in a democratic fashion.* This means that they will discuss the options in an open forum and then vote for their preferences. Using a democratic system ensures that the process will be as fair as possible. It also promotes understanding of our political system.

- *The atmosphere for choosing topics must be open, honest, and sensitive.* Students must feel comfortable in sharing their opinions. If there is any fear of teasing, ridicule, or nasty reactions, the process will not work effectively. This principle is so important that even eye rolling and groans, which may seem like standard behavior for many children, cannot be allowed. Clarify that these rules are nonnegotiable and be prepared to enforce them. Most students will welcome the move toward a more positive atmosphere.

- *In extraordinary circumstances, teachers may have to use veto power over student choices.* A student-chosen topic may possibly violate a state or district regulation. Or it may be so controversial that the school's administrators refuse to allow it. These restrictions are unfortunate because they convey the impression that students do not really have freedom. However, they also remind us that our constitutional freedoms have limits. Be sure to emphasize that such measures will be taken only in extraor-

---

- Students get to choose their topics in a democratic fashion.
- The atmosphere for choosing topics must be open, honest, and sensitive.
- In extraordinary circumstances, teachers may have to use veto power over student choices.
- Students may choose to change topics at any time.

Figure 3.2. Suggested Ground Rules

dinary circumstances and that students should not let fear of adult disapproval limit their consideration of potential topics. Even though students may express disappointment or cynicism as a result of this principle, they will still benefit from the discussion of democratic rights.

- *Students may choose to change topics at any time*. Students need reassurance that their choice of topics will not become a prison sentence. At some point, even the most interesting topic will lose its appeal. The students may have learned all they wished to know. Or perhaps the topic was not as wonderful as they had hoped. Just as with adult interests, if motivation lags, it is time to move on. There are plenty of other issues with educational value. Of course, students must give their chosen topic a reasonable amount of time before switching. Fortunately, because the topics are chosen by the students, teachers do not need to be concerned about topics being switched like the channels on the TV remote control. The decision to switch will probably be a thoughtful one because the momentum of a self-chosen unit increases as the students delve into the more interesting areas of their topic.

Once these basic ground rules are established, the class should be asked for additional rule suggestions. Whatever is proposed should be subject to discussion and a vote, but the class may want to postpone any rule decisions until they have acquired more familiarity with the process. Remind them that they may soon be confronted with problems for which a rule is needed and that new rules may be proposed at any time.

Step 3: Brainstorming Topics

Brainstorming is a method of collecting ideas in a spontaneous fashion. Ask students to suggest possible topics without regard to whether classmates or the teacher will approve. Even the most unsuitable suggestion might trigger a new idea in someone else's mind.

List all suggestions on a chart or chalkboard in the order in which they are suggested. Every idea is included, no matter how unpopular it may seem at first. After the list is complete, that original idea may be more appealing.

Save any criticism for the end of the brainstorming session. Poor ideas can be eliminated at that time. Offering immediate reactions might discourage someone from contributing because of fear of criticism. When the list is complete, we seldom remember who made which suggestion. Any criticism will, therefore, be of the idea, not the person, thus promoting honesty and avoiding the problem of anyone taking criticism personally.

It is helpful to spend a little extra time on brainstorming to be sure that students go beyond their initial ideas. When the flow of ideas becomes sluggish, prime the pump by offering your own suggestions and by encouraging topics that the students may have rejected in their heads. A good brainstorming session should result in at least two dozen suggestions.

Teachers and students who lack experience with brainstorming can benefit from using the process for other choices before embarking on curricular decision making. Students may brainstorm ideas for a bulletin board, the title of a literary magazine, or possible sources for a research project. Keep in mind that brainstorming is more than a decision-making model. It is also a good method for developing hypotheses in an inquiry lesson and interpreting works of literature and art.

Step 4: Pruning the List

With so many varied ideas, the class must narrow the list. Horticulturists prune plants to remove unhealthy limbs, thus enabling the plant to use its energy more efficiently. In student curricular decision making, we want students to ignore the weaker ideas and focus on the most appealing topics.

When pruning a tree, we must cut with care and sensitivity. A careless decision may result in a mistake, such as the removal of a healthy limb. An insensitive slice may hurt the tree itself. When pruning the list of topics, similar measures are required. This step, therefore, is divided into several parts to ensure it is done properly.

Advocacy

After the brainstorming session is completed, the teacher opens the floor for arguments, pro and con. Students are motivated to participate in this portion of the process because they know that their curricular decisions will have an impact on their immediate school lives.

Remind the students that the purpose of presenting their views is to persuade their classmates to vote the same way. A strong argument about why a particular topic is interesting, fun, or useful may convince someone else to vote for it. By the same token, effective criticism of a topic may change the vote of someone who was leaning toward that topic.

Use the discussion of this process to promote student awareness of citizens' responsibilities. The right to vote is a cornerstone of the democratic system but is inadequate, and possibly harmful, by itself. Voting must be preceded by an informed discussion of the issues. If not, a foolish decision could be made. This exercise in autonomy is a powerful strategy in developing responsible citizens.

The First Round of Voting

When discussion is complete, the first round of voting begins. In this round, students are directed to identify their top three choices of potential topics. Choosing three topics eliminates the topics that lack the support of only one or two students. It also allows the list to be substantially pruned, which is the purpose of the exercise. Limiting the choice to only one topic may result in a decision that has the support of just a portion of the class. A group of students who are interested in chess, for instance, may give the most votes to that topic, even though the rest of the class has little interest in it. The unit almost certainly would be unsuccessful.

This first-round vote can be held by silent ballot or by a show of hands. A silent ballot is better for several reasons: a) it is most akin to actual voting in a polling place, b) writing the choices on paper requires more contemplation than a mere raise of the hand, c) it is easier to make sure that students only vote for three topics, d) voters are less likely to be swayed by what their friends prefer, and e) the anonymity ensures that no one will be criticized for their choices. The only serious drawback is the time-consuming nature of silent ballots. Voting for topics is not done very often, however, and the tally of votes (if done publicly) is quite entertaining.

After the votes are tallied, the actual pruning takes place. This is when we remove less popular topics from the list. You may want to decide arbitrarily to keep the 10 most popular topics or all those receiving five or more votes. Alternatively, the class can make the decision based on their interpretation of the results. In that case, a good rule of thumb is to retain the topics that have a reasonable chance of being the ultimate choice.

More Advocacy, More Voting

From the now-reduced list, the arguments for and against particular topics should resume. This time, the matter becomes more serious as students get closer to a final decision.

When the debate dies down, students will be prepared to choose one favorite topic from the list. In this vote, however, a public show of hands is the preferred method. Each topic has received some support, so no voter is likely to be viewed as an oddball. The process is also quicker than a paper ballot.

With 10 or so topics, it is unlikely that any single one will receive a true majority. If one does, that must be the choice. If two or more topics receive substantial support, but no majority, it is time to negotiate a consensus.

Step 5: Reaching a Consensus

It may be tempting simply to hold a majority-rule final vote to settle the matter, but doing so may lead to animosity and hard feelings. That may be a good lesson in politics, but it makes for a difficult educational environment. It is better to seek a consensus in which all parties receive some satisfaction in the final choice.

One of the benefits of a public vote in the second round is that it allows the class to see which topics are preferred by which students. That knowledge lends itself to negotiation. As in a political convention, allow the students to visit with one another informally to make deals. Ask them to try to develop the plan that will make the most people happy.

Perhaps two popular topics have a common theme. If students have difficulty deciding between a unit on space travel and one on computers, a compromise unit can focus on technology. Or if the decision is between baseball and television production, the students may agree to study how baseball is televised. (Some compromises may require a bit of engineering and persuasion on the part of the teacher.)

Another kind of deal involves promises. Some students may agree to go along with the space travel unit if the others promise to support the computer unit next time. The promises can even be recorded and signed, as in the legal arena. We all know, however, that promises are often regretted, but that, too, is a good lesson for the students.

From all this negotiation, a consensus should evolve. If not, you may want to postpone making any final decisions until the following day, thus allowing further opportunity for contemplation, creative problem solving, and negotiation. If there is still no consensus, a majority-rule vote is the only alternative.

Step 6: Identifying Subthemes

Once the choice of themes is settled, ask the students to brainstorm yet again. This time, have them identify what it is about the theme they wish to know. For the most part, their initial responses to this question will determine the initial direction of the unit.

As with the earlier brainstorming session, all ideas are accepted and recorded. The more suggestions there are, regardless of their popularity, the more thinking will take place. Ideas will build upon one another until the chalkboard or chart is filled with promising directions.

Because the ideas are interrelated, the students should be able to organize them into subthemes. Ask them if any of the ideas would fit together. Younger students will need help in this classification task, but older students should easily create an organizational scheme. In a unit on zebras, for example, subtopics may include habitat, physiology, predator and prey, and value to humanity. Figure 3.3 provides additional examples of subthemes.

Expect four problems to come up during this process. First, there will be a few subtopics that fit into several categories. Remind the students that because knowledge is interrelated, almost every subtopic will present that problem. Then, encourage them to place the subtopic temporarily in what they regard as the most appropriate category until they change their minds.

Second, there will be a few subtopics that do not readily fit into a broader category, but must exist by themselves. It is fine to have a category of one, but you may also want to introduce the concept of a "miscellaneous" category. Caution the students that, like a junk drawer, the miscellaneous category sometimes becomes too crowded and disorganized, and should be used as a last resort.

Third, as the classification task is going on, new subtopics will be suggested. Allow them to be added to the list, with the observation that the planning process is never completed and that new directions will always surface.

Finally, don't despair if the process seems to take a long time. Learning is taking place not only in the form of classification skills but also as an introduction to the many facets of the theme. The very act of creating subthemes will create an advance organizer that will facilitate learning.

Another way for students to organize data is to create a curriculum web (see Figure 3.4). A web serves as a map, a graphic representation of the connections between the topics. Maps are useful for planning journeys—both educational and physical ones. Here is one way to create a curriculum web:

1. Begin by writing one topic in a circle in the center of a large piece of paper.
2. Add a related topic (from the students' list), circle it, and draw a line to connect the two.
3. Add other related topics with connecting lines.
4. Continually look for additional connections between the topics on the paper. Draw lines between them. It should eventually look like a web.
5. Do not be concerned about unusually long or crisscrossing lines. The web can always be rewritten.

Unit	Subthemes
Pets	Costs Breeds Reproduction Benefits Care of pets
Hurricanes	Weather patterns Preparedness Damage Recovery
Movies	Production Film Theaters Marketing Cultural impact
France	Language Customs Geography History Cultural arts

Figure 3.3. Units and Subthemes

Step 7: Determining the Sequence of Subthemes

Once the theme is organized into a web, or a categorical system of subthemes and topics, the next step is deciding what to study first. After wrestling with the classification process, students should have enough familiarity with the topics to be able to suggest an initial direction. In most cases, the opening topics should appear obvious. It makes sense to start with the foundations of the theme, but students

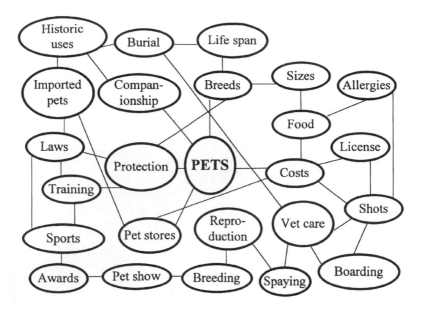

Figure 3.4. Sample Curriculum Web

may also choose to begin with the most interesting or exciting topics. It is their choice. Keep in mind that the foundations will take care of themselves. In the zebra unit, for instance, in which "predator and prey" is clearly the most exciting subtheme, the students still will learn about the zebra's physiology as part of that area of study.

Avoid the temptation to divide the class into groups so that all subthemes may be studied simultaneously. That strategy makes sense later in the school year, after you have become familiar with the students' learning styles and the students have gained some experience with the process. It is much easier to manage an innovation when everyone is working on the same topics. As questions or problems come up, the teacher and class will all be aware of them and be ready to address them. This may not happen when small groups are operating.

Once the initial subtopic has been decided, ask the students how the rest of the tentative sequence will be arranged. Directional arrows on the web may be used as a visual aid. Emphasize the tentative nature of the plan, because events will surely alter the sequence along the way. This reminder will reduce the tension in making the necessary decisions. Each of these decisions, by the way, should be determined by consensus. A majority-rule vote should be used only as a last resort.

If you can arrange it, schedule this step of the process for a Friday. (At the start of the school year, the Friday before Labor Day is ideal.) That will allow you an extra day or two to plan.

Step 8: Communicating
With Administrators and Parents

If you have not been doing so all along, this is a particularly good time to brief administrators on the students' decisions. They may have concerns about some of the topics. One or two topics may be viewed as controversial or may conflict with what another teacher is doing at a different grade level. Administrators also may have suggestions to offer regarding resources or activities. At the very least, they need to know what is being taught in the school. That's their job.

Parents also will be very interested in the forthcoming unit. They too want to be informed and will appreciate your efforts to keep them "in the loop." Besides being generally supportive, parents can suggest or provide resources that you may not have considered. They can also complement classroom lessons with relevant activities at home. If parents express any concerns about the shape or direction of the unit, those concerns can be responded to before the unit is in full swing. If compromises need to be made, the curricular adjustments can be made early and thus will be less likely to disrupt the sequence of topics.

Although administrators and parents have the right to review the curriculum and express their objections, do not expect much controversy. Almost all of the student choices will be made responsibly. Rather than express objections, the vast majority of administrators and parents will probably be impressed by the seriousness of the issues that the students have chosen and will be excited about the process. There may be complaints from parents who hold extreme views or who object to anything new or different. These individuals, although quite vocal, seldom represent anyone besides themselves. Administrators can help you measure the depth of their concerns and advise you on ways to alleviate them.

Step 9: Planning the Initial Lessons

Research

The immediate challenge for the teacher is to learn as much as possible about the topic as quickly as possible. For this reason, it is particularly helpful if the topic is already familiar. Even so, additional research will be required because knowledge changes and the students' concerns may lead to unfamiliar subtopics.

The need to do so much research in such a short time may appear daunting, and although its importance should not be underestimated, the challenge is not as difficult as it may first appear. The data collection does not have to be completed immediately. You actually have several weeks to research the topic as both you and the students gather data along the way.

The preliminary data search should focus on the starting point that the students have identified. The zebra unit, for instance, with its initial emphasis on predator and prey, requires background knowledge on that subtopic. Search for this content as you would for any other topic of personal or professional interest—use encyclopedias, textbooks, library resources, on-line requests, and the like. Unless the initial topic is unusually complex, which is unlikely as a starting point, it should be relatively easy to get a handle on it.

Expect several students to assist you voluntarily with data collection. They are apt to bring in resources that they have at home or have found in their own data searches. Encourage them to contribute to the planning process whenever possible. When students become experienced with curricular decision making, it makes sense to require their participation in planning the unit.

Of course, the resources you consult will seldom be limited to just one topic, but will probably deal with the overall theme. As you review this information, you will learn about the topic at hand as well as which resources will be most useful for the remainder of the unit. If you find the students' choice somewhat interesting, you will probably find yourself enjoying the exploration process.

Activities

As you review the content, you will no doubt be contemplating the best way for students to learn the answers to their initial questions. The simplest way, of course, is to present students with some written data that you have collected, such as a news article or encyclopedia overview. As appealing as that strategy may be, especially to a teacher or class accustomed to traditional textbook-based approaches, it is not recommended.

The first activity of a unit should be different from the usual classroom fare, reinforcing the notion of a new menu of learning experiences. An informative guest speaker, a vivid film documentary, or an intriguing set of research data will excite the students about the new unit. Be careful, however, to avoid producing such an extravagant opening activity that the rest of the unit pales in comparison. The opening activity should be more like an appetizer, stimulating the students' palates for the rest of the meal.

If possible, choose an opening activity that cannot be completed in a single day. That signals to the class that the traditional school schedule of one lesson per period is no longer operating. As students grow accustomed to their new schedule flexibility, they will begin to feel more comfortable asking questions and discussing the issues, thus promoting depth. In traditional programs, students hesitate to do so because some teachers become disconcerted when students start "taking over" the class. In this case, teachers are thrilled to pass the responsibility for learning onto the students' shoulders. An extended lesson that runs into the following day also allows more planning time.

As part of planning the initial activity, think about where it will lead. If, at the end of the activity, the class has not satisfied its interest in the initial topic, provide another perspective by using a different resource. If the first activity was the showing and discussion of a documentary film, for example, present research data as a follow-up.

If you sense that the class has completed its study of the initial topic, prepare to move on. Choose the next topic by consulting the curriculum web or category system that was used to develop the sequence. A number of alternatives should present themselves, each having distinct benefits. Make your choice based on your reading of the students' interests during the unit planning steps and, in particular, during the initial activities. Try to make the new topic a natural outgrowth of the previous one. The two topics should flow into each other in a seamless fashion, thus eliminating the need to announce a change of topics. Much like a good conversation, if the flow is truly natural, students eventually will be able to look back and trace the sequence of topics without realizing the changes that took place. This promotes the view that knowledge is truly integrated.

Purists may object, at this point, to having the teacher, rather than the students, make the choice of subsequent subtopics. Keep in mind that the students have already chosen that subtopic during the earlier steps of choosing subthemes and developing a sequence. The teacher is merely carrying out their wishes. Besides, if the flow of ideas has led naturally to the new subtopic, the teacher is not so much making a curricular decision as adapting the curriculum according to the students' interests.

Technically, the objection is accurate because, according to this model, the decision to switch topics belongs to the students. Exceptions have to be made, however, during the first week of the unit or the teacher will not have adequate time to plan the lessons properly. Remember that student curricular decision making is a process, not an event. After the first week, if planning has gone well, the teacher will then have activities for each possible change of direction. Student decision-making power will continue to increase.

Step 10: Planning the Rest of the Unit

As a result of the student planning sessions and your own research, you should be able to tentatively identify the next few subtopics that the students will choose to study. Plan the activities for those lessons as you would for any other curricular model. You may prefer to begin with behavioral objectives and then plan the lesson, or perhaps you will perform the two steps simultaneously. Either way, be sure to put your plans on paper.

Teachers who use a textbook-oriented approach tend to keep their written plans a bit vague because the textbook already identifies the objectives, content, some activities, and, occasionally, even the evaluation procedures. With student curricular decision making, your written plans do not have to be detailed, but they should include the following essential elements, listed also in Figure 3.5, that will come in handy later:

- *Objectives* tell what the students will be able to do at the end of the lesson that they were unable to do earlier. This information will guide you in developing evaluation procedures. The ob-

---

- Objectives
- Evaluation procedures
- Activities
- Prerequisites
- Cross-references

Figure 3.5. Essential Elements of a Unit Plan

jectives should relate to conceptual goals (content knowledge), process goals (thinking and other types of skills), and affective goals (feelings, values, and appreciations).

- *Evaluation procedures* measure whether the students have reached the objectives you have set. Use the same methods of preparing tests and other performance-based measurements that you have always used. Just be sure to evaluate the skill and affective goals in addition to conceptual knowledge.

- *Activities* are the strategies you use to reach the objectives and enable the students to perform the evaluation successfully. Here, too, your methods do not have to differ from your previous approach. Because the content sometimes is unavailable in textbook form, however, you may have to be creative. Many teachers find this challenge particularly refreshing. So do their students. Keep in mind that activities must meet affective and skill objectives in addition to the content goals, so a textbook-based lesson probably would be insufficient by itself.

- *Prerequisites* are the content and skills that some or all the students may lack. Third graders, for instance, may need to learn how to use the encyclopedia before researching the habitats of zebras. High schoolers probably will require some instruction in reading blueprints for their architecture unit. As activities are being planned, therefore, additional objectives will become apparent. Many of these objectives will cross subject areas as your unit gradually becomes integrated.

- *Cross-references* align the objectives with the official curriculum. Compare your list of objectives with the ones that are published by your state or district. You may be surprised how

many matches you find. Record the number of the correspond-
ing state or district objectives (e.g., Language Arts 9.4) along-
side each of your objectives. If you are a subject specialist, be
sure to consult the guidelines for other subject areas. As you
review the official list, you may notice additional objectives
that can be incorporated into your unit. Feel free to amend
your lessons appropriately, but be careful not to overload the
list. There will be room for those objectives in other units
throughout the school year.

As you record these aspects of your plans, the need for written
notes becomes obvious. The lesson objectives must be compared with
the official curriculum and also with the evaluation procedures. This
comparison is difficult to do, except in written form. Your activities
also must be aligned with the objectives and evaluation. If they do not
match, the students will have been tested on something they have not
been taught, or taught something that will not be evaluated. Both
results are harmful.

The written plans are useful in other ways, too. Evidence of
careful planning will impress those who may associate student curricular decision making with the notorious "free schools" of the
1960s. In particular, the evidence of alignment with the official curriculum will help appease skeptical parents and administrators. Furthermore, the documentation will be helpful as you evaluate your
own planning and prepare for future units. Finally, the data from your
work with student curricular decision making will be of interest to
colleagues, especially university researchers, who might wish to report on the success of the program.

Step 11: Managing the Unit

Ongoing Planning

Having tentative plans should provide a small sense of security
as you enter into the unfamiliar world of student curricular decision
making. Of course, that feeling may be shattered if student interest
galvanizes around a subtopic that you did not anticipate. Although

some teachers may feel frustrated in that situation, many others use it to remind themselves of their own limitations in anticipating student interests. The experience gives them feelings of reinforcement for putting the decision making in the hands of the students.

Most units pick up speed as they develop. As the students become acquainted with the subject matter, they will begin to bring books, news articles, videotapes, souvenirs, and a host of other relevant artifacts to class. Expect to be continually revising your plans based on these new resources. At times you may even have to alter your immediate lesson plan when you are presented with an ideal learning opportunity that cannot wait until the next day.

A unit that heavily emphasizes current events will, by necessity, continually change its shape. Ongoing developments should be monitored constantly, for they may cause your content to become outdated. The students will be sure to assist you in collecting new information (sometimes to the point of redundancy). One benefit of a current-event emphasis is the availability of special publications and television specials that offer extensive insight and analysis. These frequently offer visual images that are worth the proverbial "thousand words."

If the unit moves in a direction for which you have yet to develop plans, do not sacrifice your instructional responsibilities. There is no shame in telling the class about the unexpected nature of their decisions. Older students, in particular, will take pride in their unpredictability. Teachers have every right to declare a brief moratorium to prepare additional lessons. Doing so makes educational sense, too.

Such a change of direction provides a good time to review and summarize the unit up to that point. As they review, students may identify questions that have gone unanswered, related topics that have yet to be explored, and previously studied issues that require clarification. Summarizing allows students to exercise creativity in presenting what they have learned to each other or to the rest of the school. This is a good time to develop such synthesizing activities and materials as bulletin boards, news articles, plays, and other artistic representations of their newfound knowledge. At the conclusion of synthesis, exams and other forms of evaluation may take place. All of these activities take time, which allows the teacher to prepare new lesson plans.

Student Behavior

Because student decision making may be associated with free-dom and empowerment, students may get the false signal that stan-dards are being lowered and that "anything goes." Teachers must take care to disabuse them of that notion.

Freedom and empowerment require more, not less, responsibility on the students' part. The students no longer can claim lack of interest for their failure to behave in class or to complete homework assign-ments. When they behave irresponsibly, they are not just disappoint-ing their teacher but also letting down their fellow students, who have made a group decision to work together. Self-control, therefore, is essential.

Although this idea is worthy of a teacher lecture, like most impor-tant lessons, it is best learned through experience. Expect students to test the limits of the new system. When the inevitable irresponsible behavior occurs, enforce the rules swiftly and effectively (using the same disciplinary system you have used all along) to make a state-ment that standards will not be relaxed. At the same time, encourage students to help each other develop skills in self-control so that they may continue to gain freedom.

The one type of misbehavior that must be carefully monitored is linked to boredom. If you sense that students are tiring of the topic, it may be time to move on. Perhaps they have learned all they wish to know about the topic or are more interested in something else. If you suspect that this change is occurring, confront it. Tell the class what you have observed and solicit their opinions. Their misbehavior may be a reaction to a particular activity or subtopic and not to the unit itself. Or there may be some other cause of student inattention. After all, they have so much going on in their lives. The best approach is to ask them directly.

Step 12: Concluding the Unit

The decision to conclude a unit does not mean that all activities are instantly suspended. On the contrary, it sets several wheels in motion.

First, decisions have to be made concerning which subtopics will be further explored and which will go unstudied. The class may decide to switch to a new unit as soon as possible, or they may designate a particular subtopic as the final one. They may even decide to set an arbitrary ending date, particularly if it falls just before a holiday or the end of the semester.

Second, ongoing projects, such as research reports and creative activities, must be completed and scheduled for presentation. It is tempting for the students, in anticipation of exciting changes, to begin rushing through their projects in an urge to move on. Remind them that doing so would result in dissatisfaction on the part of parents, teachers, and, especially, themselves.

Third, planning for a new unit must begin. That decision brings us back to Step 3, Brainstorming Topics, unless the previous negotiations already have determined the next unit topic. Even so, the decision should be subject to review. The class probably will choose to honor its commitments, but it also may recognize that conditions have changed and that their earlier decision no longer makes as much sense. At this point, some of the negotiators may cry foul. Allow the students to discuss this ethical issue and discuss how it applies to other agreements and contracts in the social and business worlds.

When the class has chosen its new topic, it obviously will be necessary for the teacher to begin another cycle of planning. This time, however, the planning process should be a lot easier due to familiarity with the students, the process, and the resources. If the new unit topic is one that had been chosen as part of the previous negotiations, you probably already will have several resources available.

Finally, the decision to end a unit calls for summary and review activities, such as those discussed in the previous step. In this case, a more substantial synthesizing activity is in order. A culminating activity should be more than a summarizing session; it should be a celebratory event. A strong culminating activity reminds the students of what they have accomplished and will motivate them to work equally hard in subsequent units.

The product of the culminating activity should highlight what was learned in the unit, so that interested observers will get a solid grasp of what your class has accomplished. This understanding will be useful in maintaining support for the process. A class magazine, for example, that includes reports on each of the subtopics that the class studied may impress skeptics at the same time it serves as a souvenir for the students and their friends and family. A stage, screen, or television production would also serve this purpose. If possible, include an authors' party or a cast party for the students and their guests. Let them know that developing their own unit has been a great achievement. If some of the spotlight is reflected onto you, enjoy it. You deserve a lot of credit!

Step 13: Reflect, Revise, and Publicize

As one unit ends and another begins, it is easy to become so absorbed in planning for the next unit that you abandon the old one. Take the time to conclude the unit in a professional manner. It is an investment that will pay off in the future.

Reflect

Sit back and review the elements of the unit. Consider the steps you followed in developing the unit. Most of the following questions should be pertinent:

- How did it evolve?
- How did the original design compare to actual curriculum?
- Were there any surprises?
- What problems did you and the class experience?
- What insights have you gotten from the topic?
- What insights have you gotten from your students?
- What insights have you gotten about your teaching?
- What will you do differently in the next unit?

These questions may require time to compose thoughtful, complex answers. Therefore, this step should not be rushed. To maximize results, it is best to use more than one session to conduct your review.

Many teachers mentally review their work when they are alone, such as in the car or in the bathtub. Although solitude is an important factor, those sites seldom allow for any written notes. Any great realizations may never be recorded under those circumstances.

A written review is much more effective. Journal writing promotes a depth of reflection and processing that seldom can be achieved in other ways. Each time you review your entries, whether it is while you are writing, immediately after, the next day, or the next year, your written comments will provide insight and, occasionally, catharsis.

Revise

Forcing yourself to review the unit will no doubt lead you to several strengths and weaknesses. They are both worth noting in your journal or on the planning sheets themselves.

If you do this unit again, or perhaps use one or more subtopics, you will want to capitalize on its strengths. Noting which activities provided substantial excitement or a slew of student questions will be useful information the next time that topic or subtopic becomes the focus.

Weaknesses are another matter. We prefer to forget about them, but it is far better to revise the unit. Inadequate resources, poor lessons, or weak test questions should be corrected while the review is fresh. Leaving it for another time may result in no revision at all, and the topic surely will resurface later when planning time is tightest, resulting in a shoddy revision. Or, if you forget all about the revisions, your new unit will remain weak. Take the time to do it well.

Publicize

A revised unit plan is a valuable resource. Other teachers may want to use parts of it in their own classrooms. Your principal may wish to share portions of it in a parent meeting or with other administrators. University professors might like copies to distribute to prospective teachers. Perhaps the school district would like to publicize it as a sample of the innovative teaching that takes place in the local schools.

(I am particularly interested in communicating with educators who have tried these ideas or developed similar ones. Any letters, phone calls, faxes, or e-mail will be appreciated. Graduate students and other educational researchers who are interested in studying this model are welcome to any and all of the data. Please contact me.)

Although many teachers prefer to be humble about their achievements, publicity is a necessary evil. Parents, citizens, and fellow educators all need to be convinced of the value of students choosing school content. A finished product can convince them of the model's merits. It may inspire potential allies to use the process themselves. At the very least, it will get people to talk about the idea. Publicizing your unit will counter the first objection that is usually made to student curricular decision making: "It's a nice idea, but it won't work." It *can* work, and it is your responsibility to spread the word.

4

Student Curricular
Decision Making in Action

Introduction

In 1990, after 10 years of teaching at the college level, I had a strong desire to return to the K–12 classroom. Although my work as both a junior high social studies teacher and an elementary school teacher had served me well at the university level, I needed more experience. I constantly used what I had learned as a K–12 teacher in my work as a methods professor, writer, researcher, and consultant, but my new ideas were no longer correlated with my experiences.

Professors are constantly studying. Like all teachers, we must become well-acquainted with the content we teach, as well as with new ideas that are presented in professional journals and conferences. In addition, to conduct research and write in our areas of specialty, we must become relative experts. It is our responsibility, when we speak or put something in print, to be sure it is valid and reliable. We must study our topics carefully.

I had been studying the field of curriculum when I first became aware of student curricular decision making. As I became more and more convinced of its theoretical value, I felt the urge to translate theory into practice. Doing so would provide more than personal or professional satisfaction; it would allow me to learn more about the model. Is it truly effective? What problems do teachers face when they implement the model? How can those constraints be overcome? In exploring the literature, I discovered that the research base on this topic was scant. I was eager to try this approach myself.

I recently had volunteered to teach a course for one semester at a public open middle school in Charlotte, North Carolina. This school was one of two magnet schools among the 22 middle schools in the district. Its magnet status meant that families applied by lottery to attend this school, which was designated to adhere to the "open school" concept. Of all the area schools, I believed this one would be most amenable to alternative methods of education.

The administrators of the school eagerly supported my request. Due to scheduling considerations that limited my time in the school, the principal recommended that I teach one of the school's dozens of elective classes. (Available electives included chorus, drama, computers, and the school newspaper.) Given the opportunity to design an elective, I formulated a one-period class on current events (titled "Current Issues"), reflecting one of my scholarly interests.

The class was assigned to the art room, which was free during first period. This location turned out to be quite fortunate.

Fifteen students enrolled in the class, which was about average for elective classes at the middle school. After numerous additions and deletions during the drop-add period, eleven students remained— five white boys, one African American boy, three African American girls, and two white girls. These ratios were similar to the school's racial and gender composition. Students' self-reported data indicated that they enrolled for a variety of reasons, including interest in current issues, parental pressure, the appeal of having a university professor as a teacher, and, most often, because they did not know what else to take. Except for two eighth graders, all were ninth graders.

The First Week

On the first day, I introduced myself and my plan to the class. I told them that they would be determining the curriculum for the course. Any content was fine, I told them, as long as it was a current issue. Because practically any topic has controversial elements, this was not much of a limitation. I asked them to think about possible topics for us to consider. We would discuss the possibilities during the week and make a decision when we felt the time was right. The class was extremely enthusiastic, especially about the idea of approaching controversial subjects.

Before making their momentous curricular decision, I wanted the students to get to know each other, acquire a taste of how the class would work, and observe my teaching style. These preliminary goals would make the decision-making process go smoother. They also would allow me time to plan the initial lessons.

The Soviet leader, Mikhail Gorbachev, had been kidnapped the previous weekend. This was a familiar topic to me, requiring minimal preparation. It also appeared to interest the students (it's not every day that a world leader gets kidnapped), so I suggested we study events in the Soviet Union until we got the new unit off the ground.

Because major developments were occurring on a daily basis, each class session that first week began with a review and discussion of the events in Moscow. We watched news reports that I had video-taped the previous evening, then the floor was opened for discussion. As I expected, the students had little knowledge of Russian history or communism.

To relieve their confusion, I presented materials about the Soviet Union from news magazines and textbooks, which I supplemented with personal tales of my childhood during the Cold War. I assigned the students to interview their parents and grandparents for other anecdotes. We learned about Czarist Russia, the 1917 revolution, and the regimes of Lenin, Stalin, Kruschev, Brezhnev, and Gorbachev. When the Soviet Union was reconfigured into a commonwealth of independent states, we conducted a simulated meeting of the 16 republics. All of this planning required a lot of work on my part, after school hours, but it was worth it. The students were enjoying the variety of methods, becoming comfortable with expressing their opinions, and learning a great deal about European and American foreign policy.

Planning the First Student-Directed Unit

In addition to studying events in Moscow, part of each class session was devoted to planning. Topic selection began late in the first week with brainstorming. Figure 4.1 lists the proposed topics in the order in which they were suggested.

After we listed the topics on the chalkboard, the class discussed the advantages of any topics that interested them. Some of the advantages that were cited included relevance, access to local sources, high

Violence	Date rape
War	Sexually transmitted diseases
Racial conflict	Censorship
South Africa	Homelessness
Religious conflicts	Poverty
Environment	Gangs
USSR	Child abuse
Drugs	Elderly abuse
Teen pregnancy	Domestic violence

Figure 4.1. List of Brainstormed Topics—First Round

interest, and the absence of the topic in the rest of their classes. During this discussion, the students got to gauge their classmates' preferences. I wanted the class to make a thoughtful decision, so I postponed the vote until the next day. I also (correctly) anticipated that the class leaders would be organizing support for their favorite topics during lunch and on the buses.

The next day, a vote was held in which each student could vote for three topics. The only topics that received votes were teenage pregnancy, abortion, and gangs (a distant third). I could not help noting that these were topics that had immediate relevance to teenage life.

Rather than vote again, which would result in disgruntled losers, I urged the students to negotiate. They were allowed to walk around the room and talk to each other about their preferences. After that, I told them, we would have a final ballot in which each student had a single vote.

After a period of frenzied negotiation, they proudly announced that a vote would not be necessary—they had reached a compromise. Rather than decide between the top two choices, the class had chosen to study teen pregnancy and incorporate the topic of abortion. The advocates of studying gangs supported the compromise when they recognized that they did not have enough votes. The parallels to modern political life did not escape me.

What problems do pregnant teens have—economic, health, and social?

What programs are offered in the community for pregnant teens?

Which groups have the highest percentages of teen pregnancies—race, class, location?

What percentage of fathers stay with the mother?

Is there a higher incidence of child abuse among teenage parents?

What are the long-term effects of a teenage pregnancy?

Why do teenage pregnancies occur?

What problems are likely for children of teenage parents?

What are the public costs of teenage pregnancies?

What ages are most likely to become pregnant?

What options does each age choose?

Figure 4.2. Students' Questions Regarding Teenage Pregnancy

I confessed to the students that I did not have a deep knowledge of the topic of teenage pregnancy. To help me prepare, I needed to know what specific questions they had. We then brainstormed a list of subtopics, listed in Figure 4.2.

I was impressed by the thoughtfulness of the students' questions. I was also pleased that the answers probably would be readily available as well as interesting. I promised the class that I would begin my planning that day, but in the meantime we had some unfinished business.

Finishing the Unit on Russia

I had to make sure that the class was ready to move on from the study of Russia. (This topic had started off as a study of the Soviet Union, and I was certain that these students would never again confuse the two.) The students diplomatically assured me that they had enjoyed the unit, but said that it was becoming a bit boring. In other words, the topic was more my choice than theirs. We agreed to conclude the unit that week, so I scheduled an exam for Friday.

I found it harder than usual to design this test. After all, the content I taught had been changing every day. When the unit started, I did not expect to be teaching about Russian history or civil wars. I had to review my lesson plans and reconceptualize my objectives. Once I did that, it was relatively easy to design an essay exam. It tested the students on their ability to

1. Describe the impact of communism on the Soviet people, on life in the United States, and on the rest of the world
2. Identify how each of the following would react to the fall of communism: Soviet military leaders, Russian peasants, leaders of the Baltic republics, and President Bush
3. Explain how historical, economic, and geographic characteristics contributed to the current state of affairs

I was pleased with the results of the essay exam. In the entire class, only one student scored below a B. The average grade was B+. Even more impressive was the depth of understanding reflected in the answers. I felt it reinforced my decision to move away from a textbook-based program.

The Teen Pregnancy Unit

Planning

To plan the new unit, I needed resources to provide a knowledge base. I decided to examine the public and school library collections and consult a professor of health education. The libraries did not have any books that specifically addressed the students' questions. There were some journal articles available, however.

The health education professor was a gold mine. She had several textbooks and several class activities to offer. One textbook included a series of case studies detailing the lives of pregnant teenagers. These stories involved a variety of ethnic groups that cut across income levels. Each story had a different outcome (e.g., adoption, abortion, keeping the child). Having the students read these stories would introduce the topic in an interesting fashion before moving on to the more technical issues. Journal entries in which the students reacted to the case studies would help the students organize their ideas for class discussion and assist me in getting to know them better.

For statistical information, the health professor referred me to the county agency that deals with adolescent pregnancy. Local data would be most effective because it could make the unit more relevant and interesting. The agency had a vast collection of brochures, video-tapes, press releases, and books.

Knowing that reading and discussing the case studies would take a few days, I had time to sort through the data. I discovered answers to most of the students' questions. Content knowledge was only one of my goals, however. I also wanted to develop student skills in reading, interpreting, and analyzing research reports. Rather than present the information to the students, I decided to let them do the processing themselves. I had them choose the questions they wished to answer, form small groups, help each other figure out what things meant, and prepare a presentation to the rest of the class.

Administrative Consultation

To my surprise, during all these introductory lessons, the school's administrators had not come to observe. Surely my status as a new-comer trying an experimental curriculum would invite at least a cursory inspection. I figured that the administrators were distracted by the usual bureaucratic hassles that bedevil every school in September. It was also possible that they had total faith in me. Just the same, I knew that the topic of teenage pregnancy was sufficiently controversial so that they needed to be informed. I therefore wrote a note to the assistant principal, telling him about the unit.

He was waiting by my classroom first thing in the morning. The administration did have concerns: Parents might not have been ex-pecting a study of teenage pregnancy in a class about current issues. The content might conflict with the new sex-education program. Plus, the conservative school board member who objected to the sex-education program might decide to make a fuss.

Meeting with the administrators and presenting the students' questions helped to relieve their concerns. The art teacher was also helpful in providing an objective voice. It became clear that the unit really was not going to be about sexuality but about social issues. The administrators were still hesitant to approve the unit, however, because of their sensitivity to political pressures. They called the area superintendent, who reviewed the unit plans (thank goodness they were carefully done), and declared the unit acceptable. The one stipulation was that I send a letter to the students' parents that identified the unit topics and asked for feedback.

The letter was sent the following day. All feedback was positive. Parents were thrilled to have their children learning about the consequences of teen pregnancy. The unit was on!

Class Sessions

Each class session was divided between small-group research sessions for the first half of class and, afterwards, a whole-class discussion of the case studies. I met periodically with each group to facilitate their independent studies. Some groups needed a lesson in interpreting statistics that were presented in table form. The more independent workers merely had to be directed toward rich data sources. Only the students using the video encyclopedia in the media center had trouble staying on task. They were distracted by the other provocative topics in that resource. I resolved to put the groups together more carefully next time.

The case studies provoked significant discussion. Although I had not originally planned it that way, when we confronted an intriguing issue (e.g., causes of teen pregnancies), one of the small groups usually was able to provide additional information. Once I was convinced that the class had sufficient background knowledge from the case-study discussions, it was time for the presentations.

During the presentations, the students paid careful attention to each other and asked thoughtful questions. I was particularly pleased to see them becoming comfortable with statistical data. They appeared to be proud of their independence in researching, designing, and presenting such relevant data.

New Subtopics

From time to time, the discussion began to move away from the original topic. When it did, I attempted to provide activities for the new direction. For instance, teenage pregnancy and its social consequences evolved into a discussion of adoption when that option came up in the case studies. We examined local adoption services and explored some of the legal issues regarding rights of the birth parents, adoptive parents, and child.

When abortion was being discussed, we changed direction again. At the time, the antiabortion group Operation Rescue was demonstrating in Wichita, Kansas, so abortion protests became the focus. A number of students expressed interest in the general topic of civil disobedience. I then gathered materials and designed activities to meet that demand. Although the topic changes were often stressful for me, the new topics were always interesting enough to make it intellectually compelling, so I did not mind the extra work. The complete sequence of topics is shown in Figure 4.3.

When attention appeared to be waning, or if specific complaints were expressed, the students were reminded that the decision about when to move to a new topic was strictly theirs. The students made that choice at the end of their Supreme Court discussion, thus ending their study of teenage pregnancy and abortion. They then voted to move to the topic of teenage gangs. This had been their unspoken intention earlier in the semester, but they formally engaged in brainstorming and voting just to be sure.

The Culminating Activity

The class had to complete the teenage pregnancy unit before studying gangs. We had learned a great deal about pregnancy, adoption, and abortion, I told them. Was there some way we could share it? I encouraged the students to think about how to educate the rest of the school but still be entertaining.

The next day I was absent and the art teacher took my place. Under her guidance, the class decided to create a videotape about teenage pregnancy that could air over the school's closed-circuit

1. Teenage pregnancy
2. Societal consequences
3. Adoption
4. Legal issues re: adoption
5. Abortion
6. Civil disobedience
7. State legislation re: abortion
8. The state judicial system
9. Supreme Court
10. Prohibition
11. Mobsters
12. Drug trade
13. Teenage gangs in L.A.
14. Turf
15. Urban geography
16. Guns
17. Gun control
18. Violence
19. Sex differences re: violence
20. Television's influence on violence
21. Family influences on socialization
22. Sex roles
23. TV censorship
24. Bill of Rights

Figure 4.3. Flow of Topics

television system. Having had experience with student drama, I welcomed the idea when I heard about it the following day.

We had recently discussed scripts, acting, and video techniques during our study of abortion when the class watched the made-for-television movie, *Roe vs. Wade.* (This may have been the impetus for their decision.) It was, therefore, an easy transition into the topic of dramatic production. The students brainstormed plot ideas, then each was assigned to write a creative story for homework.

The next day, the students read each other's stories and chose the one that they felt would best present what they had learned. They selected a story about an interracial teenage couple who receive conflicting advice on dealing with an unexpected pregnancy. At the end of the story, after a bitter fight between the lovers, the girl has an abortion to spite her boyfriend. It was an effective way to show that teenagers often lack the maturity to deal with the consequences of premarital sex.

Rather than develop a script, the class improvised the scenes until they felt right. Ultimately, the improvisations turned into rehearsals, with each student settling into a part. We practiced it as a play for a day or two, then moved into the television studio. Fortunately, one of the students regularly served as a camera operator for the morning announcements, so we had him teach us how to operate the cameras. We experimented with camera angles, fades, set design, credits, music, and other technical problems as they arose.

Choosing a title was not simple. We analyzed titles of movies, books, and television shows to better understand the characteristics of an effective title. The students then brainstormed their own titles for the production. After critiquing each other's ideas, they voted for "The Young and the Pregnant."

An advertising campaign followed. The class examined collections of movie posters and analyzed their appeal. They then designed their own posters and displayed them around the school. Having access to the art room was very helpful in this project.

I was delighted not only with the students' creativity but even more with the feelings of common purpose that had arisen. The videotape was a successful production that also helped the students synthesize what they had learned. To measure their achievement, I created an essay test that would have them explain the options available to a pregnant teenager; analyze the consequences of teen pregnancy from personal, family, and societal perspectives; and discuss how pregnant teens are affected by the legislative and judicial processes. Results were outstanding. Every student in the class had a C or higher. The average grade was B.

The Unit on Gangs

Getting Started

I began my inquiry into the topic of gangs during the time the class worked on its videotape production. Not knowing much about gangs, I consulted the *New York Times Index*, *Sociological Abstracts*, and various other information services to gather data. It was during this research that I discovered how gangs, or mobs, evolved from bootleggers taking advantage of the ban on alcohol during Prohibition. I seized upon that as an entrée to the new unit. Prohibition resulted from a constitutional amendment, thus relating the topic directly to the previous unit's focus on the Supreme Court's role in determining whether laws are constitutional. I also believed that the colorful events of the 1920s would be appealing to the students.

The lesson began with an overview of the situation. Through question-and-answer techniques, I helped the students analyze the economic situation that made bootlegging so profitable. Before I had the chance to ask, the students made the connection between alcohol prohibition and the current ban on narcotics. This discussion was enhanced by the contribution of the art teacher, who told the story of her uncle, who smuggled liquor from Canada to Detroit. The students were fascinated by the similarities between bootlegging and current-day drug smuggling. They had not anticipated the connection between teenage gangs and drug trafficking, and were pleasantly surprised to be examining yet another relevant topic that was seldom discussed in classrooms.

Students continued studying the development of gangs the following day by reading an article from *The New York Times Magazine* about a current-day mobster who was testifying about mob activity. This article, which I discovered in my research, was extremely well written and chilling in its descriptions of gang violence and intrigue. The class silently read a portion of the article and then discussed both the content and journalist's literary skill. This was part of my constant effort to integrate school subjects wherever possible.

After concluding the article, the students appeared to have enough of an overview to choose the direction of the teenage gang unit. I asked them what they wanted to know and led a brainstorming session of possible subtopics. After a lengthy discussion, students chose to explore why people join gangs, the role of females in gangs, the racial and ethnic composition of gangs, how much money is involved, and levels of violence.

Independent Work

Students had the option of working alone or in pairs, and all chose to have partners. (This time I made sure that each pair had at least one responsible member.) Each team chose its topic and made tentative plans, in consultation with me, concerning possible data sources and the types of presentations they would make to the rest of the class.

Having already checked the school library's collection, I recognized its limitations and collected the relevant articles for the students from the university library. These were distributed to the groups at the following class session. The students read the articles (I assisted them with challenging jargon) and prepared their presentations.

The presentations were of varying quality. One group performed a brief skit that detailed their findings, while another group read from garbled notes. One presentation in particular that caught the students' attention dealt with the concept of "turf." I followed through by presenting a brief introduction to urban geography, a subject I had studied in college.

An Unexpected Set of Activities

The students, all of whom lived in the inner city or traveled through it to school each morning, were stimulated by the similarities between their own city and the classic urban model of concentric circles representing different economic zones. I seized upon their interest by allowing them to draw maps of fictional cities and encouraging them to identify prime gang turf on the maps.

As I looked at the students' maps, they reminded me of the boards used in the games Risk® and Life®. That inspired me to suggest using the maps to create a board game on gangs. Although some students expressed skepticism about the practicality of the idea, most responded enthusiastically to the opportunity to creatively extend their learning.

The class then brainstormed characteristics of successful board games and, in small groups, tried to apply them to their own maps. Each group then shared their game rules with the rest of the class for feedback. Two approaches appeared to be particularly popular, so I let them choose which game version they wanted to work with and then plan the subsequent steps in producing the games, including the game pieces, cards, and artwork.

Local Application

As this activity was going on, the students expressed continued interest in the history and current presence of gangs in the local community. They suggested that they interview the police officer assigned to the school for community relations. I made that arrangement and also invited a representative from the local drug education center, who was recognized for her knowledge of gang activity, to visit at a later date. Time was set aside to prepare interview questions and plan ways to share the knowledge with the rest of the school.

The police interview began in a provocative manner when the officer argued that the city did not have any gang activity. This contradicted the students' own experiences and stimulated significant discussion. When the drug education center representative appeared, they asked her about the officer's statement. She disagreed with the officer and explained that the police have developed criteria for determining whether a crime is gang related that tend to underestimate the level of gang activity and, therefore, make the police appear more effective. The students were delighted by her candor and engaged in extensive discussion of the causes and implications of the police misrepresentations. This discussion evolved into an examination of gang violence, access to guns, and gun control, which consumed much of the following few weeks.

Culminating Activities

The unit would have evolved further, but the semester was nearing an end. Because there was little time remaining for a major culminating activity, I sought a synthesizing activity that would be simpler than a videotape production.

I had the students create editorial cartoons concerning gangs. We examined cartoons from a variety of newspapers, identifying how the cartoonists used humor and exaggeration to make their points. In so doing, we could not help discussing the current events that the cartoons depicted. The discussions inspired the students to develop very clever cartoons of their own.

After the students presented the cartoons to each other, I gave an essay test to measure whether the students had reached the unit objectives. The test items asked for an analysis of why people join gangs, the role of females in gangs, the racial and ethnic composition of gangs, how much money is involved, and levels of violence. These were the very questions the students identified at the beginning of the unit.

Student performance on the exam was strong. This left me with a positive feeling about the relationship between achievement and student curricular decision making. I was even more gratified when the research data that had been collected by one of my colleagues were made available to me at the end of the course. That report is presented in the next chapter, along with other research findings.

5

Covering Required Content and Other Curricular Goals

Covering Content

Teachers are under enormous pressure to "cover" the curriculum. State mandates, district policies, and especially standardized tests have forced many teachers to rush through the required content, despite substantial evidence that doing so results in a lack of student motivation, interest, and long-term learning (Passe, 1995).

Clearly, there is not enough time in the school day or year to adequately address all of the required topics. In the meantime, new content is constantly added while student time in class is steadily being reduced.

In the midst of this conundrum comes a new approach to curriculum planning that passes decision making into the students' hands. How can we possibly cover the curriculum under these circumstances?

Surprisingly, I discovered it is not that difficult. Using my notes from the current issues class described in the previous chapter, I compared the North Carolina curriculum guide for 9th-grade social studies (North Carolina Department of Public Instruction, 1985) to my students' self-selected curriculum.

My analysis shows substantial correlation. The North Carolina curriculum guide identifies 15 knowledge goals and 8 skills goals that are to govern social studies instruction in that grade level. Figure 5.1 provides a matrix of each goal and shows whether it was met by the student-chosen curriculum.

North Carolina Goals (Content)	Topics Chosen by Students That Met the Goal
1. Have a continuous awareness and understanding of issues and problems confronting the economic, legal, and political system.	All course topics included analysis from the standpoint of economic, legal, and political issues.
2. Know the responsibilities associated with citizenship.	Civil disobedience, community social services, the judicial system, the legislative process, the Bill of Rights. Each topic included some discussion of citizen rights and responsibilities.
3. Know that scarcity causes individuals and groups to make economic choices.	Prohibition, gun control, the drug trade, community social services, adoption. Each topic addressed the economic advantages and disadvantages of natural or artificial shortages.
4. Know that the United States has a free enterprise economic system.	Prohibition, the drug trade, guns, television. In each of these topics, students discussed whether governmental control violates the principle of free enterprise.
5. Know the relationship between economic goals and social values.	Prohibition, gun control, the drug trade, television censorship. In each topic, students addressed the trade-off between social values and economics.
6. Know the characteristics of command, market, and mixed economies.	Turmoil in eastern Europe. As they analyzed the transition of the USSR to a market economy, students worked with all three concepts.

Figure 5.1. State Guidelines and How They Were Met by the Student-Chosen Curriculum

North Carolina Goals (Content)	Topics Chosen by Students That Met the Goal
7. Know the basic factors of production (land, labor, capital, and entrepreneurial skills).	Turmoil in eastern Europe, the drug trade, prohibition. In analyzing the success and failure of these economies and industries, students used these concepts.
8. Know that there is disagreement as to the role of government in the economy.	Prohibition, gun control, the drug trade, television censorship. Students debated the role of government as they discussed each of these topics.
9. Know the function of money and financial institutions in the American economy.	Mob activity, the drug trade, gang wars. The use of loan sharks, laundered money, and investment capital was a central element of these topics.
10. Know why we live in a society governed by law.	Legal issues regarding adoption, abortion, the Supreme Court, mob activity, gangs, the drug trade, gun control, violence, the Bill of Rights. The role of law (and unlawfulness) was a major issue with these topics.
11. Know the importance of the roles of the United States and North Carolina constitutions.	Supreme Court, the state judicial system, the Bill of Rights. Students confronted constitutional mandates as they explored each of these topics.
12. Know the structure and function of the American government under law.	The legislative process, the judicial system, the Bill of Rights. Students studied the structure and function of government in their study of these topics.

(continued)

North Carolina Goals (Content)	Topics Chosen by Students That Met the Goal
13. Know how conflicts and disputes are addressed by the legal and political systems.	The legislative process, the judicial system, the Bill of Rights, the Supreme Court. Students explored the legal and political systems extensively with reference to abortion rights, gun control, Prohibition, and gangs.
14. Know the roles and functions of officials and agencies in the legal and judicial system.	The legislative process, the judicial system, the Bill of Rights, the Supreme Court. Students studied the structure and function of government officials and agencies in their study of these topics.
15. Know how to function in a democratic society.	The legislative process, the judicial system, the Bill of Rights, the Supreme Court, civil disobedience. The principle of democracy was an essential element of these topics.
North Carolina Goals (Skills)	Activities That Promoted Those Skills
16. Identify and define problems and suggest ways of solving them.	Consideration of each course topic.
17. Locate and gather needed information.	Research on community social services, adoption requirements, consequences of teenage pregnancy; articles on mob activity, the drug trade, gun control; guest speakers on gangs and guns.

Figure 5.1. Continued

North Carolina Goals (Skills)	Activities That Promoted Those Skills
18. Evaluate information.	Examination of all materials described above with regard to validity, reliability, and bias.
19. Organize and analyze information and draw conclusions.	Consideration of each course topic, involving student research and presentations that required these skills.
20. Use maps and globes.	Extensive use of maps in studying turmoil in eastern Europe and urban geography.
21. Have a sense of time and chronology.	Turmoil in eastern Europe, *Roe v. Wade*, Prohibition, mobsters: analysis of each of these topics using time-lines and other chronological considerations.
22. Demonstrate growth in self-management.	Choosing topics, conducting research, preparing presen-tations, organizing debates—activities requiring indepen-dent work habits.
23. Participate effectively in groups.	Extensive discussion, debate, simulation, negotiation, and compromise for all course activities.

Figure 5.1. Continued

All 23 goals were addressed, in varying degrees, by the one-semester curriculum. A standard two-semester course would no doubt yield greater depth and practice in relation to each goal. This finding indicates that meeting the curricular goals is not only achiev-able, but possibly easier, when students make the curricular choices. An examination of these contributing factors will clarify the point.

Efficiency Factors

FEWER INTRODUCTORY AND REVIEW LESSONS

Many elementary-school social studies teachers, for example, spend a great deal of time introducing and reviewing map and globe skills. I have observed latitude and longitude units that took 2 weeks to teach. Map and globe skills are emphasized, usually at the beginning of the year, because they are foundations for later learning. (Teachers who closely follow the text tend to teach map skills first because textbooks usually begin with them.) Unfortunately, when it comes time to use those skills, students are likely to require additional instruction and review. This frustrating process occurs in other grade levels and curricular areas too, such as with grammar in the English class, the periodic table of elements in science, and basic arithmetic in math.

Time-consuming review becomes necessary when students do not get to apply the skills to any meaningful content. Exercises at the beginning of the book tend to be based on arbitrary content and are viewed as busywork. In addition, the time period between initial instruction and the ultimate application lesson could be several months.

In a student-chosen curriculum, skills are taught in context. When a student needs to use latitude, predicate phrases, or the atomic structure of carbon, the teacher provides opportunities to grasp the concept and instantly apply it. The learning process is significantly more efficient.

LACK OF INTEREST IN MINOR TOPICS AND SKILLS

Most educators will agree that all content is not of equal importance. Yet we often emphasize certain topics excessively. It is a rare elementary school teacher, for example, that does not have a unit on the Pilgrims. It has gotten to the point that our students have become experts on this minor historical period. They can create Pilgrim hats, plan a Thanksgiving menu, and recite the poem about the *Mayflower*. Yet these same students might lack knowledge of such 20th-century events as the Korean conflict and Watergate because there was not enough time to cover them in class. There is a similar overemphasis on several other topics, such as the spelling of unusual words, division of fractions, and plant structure.

These topics are overemphasized for a variety of reasons. Teachers may be more comfortable with simple, familiar, or favorite topics, or they may need help in allocating curricular time. In some cases, teachers prefer activities that are easy to plan and manage, or they believe students want and need more work on the topic.

Whatever the reason, students seldom will make similar curricular decisions on their own. As it turns out, they will choose more important content and skills that are likely to appear on the state guidelines. The initial choices they make will reflect their interests and needs, and then they will move on to other meaningful topics. This process avoids overemphasizing insignificant content and promotes efficiency.

MORE EFFICIENT LEARNING

In traditional curricular models, teachers must constantly provide experiences in which students practice using a particular skill or remembering what they have learned. This happens when students are unmotivated to learn the subject in the first place. The process becomes time consuming and quite boring.

One key advantage of student-centered curricular decision making is its superiority in motivating students. When students are eager to learn content or skills, they are less likely to forget what they have learned. They will immediately apply the knowledge or skill, thus promoting long-term retention. Time pressure is reduced.

CORRELATION WITH STANDARDIZED TESTS AND CURRICULUM GUIDES

The North Carolina social studies objectives may appear surprising because of their lack of specificity, but North Carolina is not alone. Several other states have rewritten their goals to reflect the recent movement away from ultraspecific content goals. The common perception that schools are required to teach traditional facts is no longer accurate. Although several rather specific goals remain on the books, examples such as the ones below are becoming more and more typical.

- English, Grades 5-8: Students analyze how new words enter languages and how meanings evolve over time (Massachusetts).

- Mathematics, K-4: Students construct, read, and interpret displays of data including tables, charts, pictographs, and bar graphs (Colorado).
- Science, middle level: Students debate various theories of the formation of the universe (Florida).
- Arts, high school: Students analyze their own and others' artistic products and performances using accepted standards (Kentucky).
- World languages, high school: Students understand, interpret, and produce appropriate gestures, facial expressions, and body language (Michigan).

Such broad goals reduce the pressure on teachers to emphasize traditional content that consumes substantial portions of classroom time. We no longer have to spend hours instructing, practicing, and testing students on their ability to memorize classic poems, names of presidents, or bones in the body. The meaning of the poems, the impact of certain presidents, and the relevance of particular bones are what is taught—and what is likely to be remembered. Along the way, students may choose to memorize portions of a classic poem, not for the test, but because they enjoy reciting a poem that has meaning to them. Memorizing names of bones is useful only for a career in health or medicine. Everyone else needs to know only the major ones. And those, like the names of presidents, are best learned as part of a higher cognitive goal, learning for understanding.

The end-of-year tests, which are based on the official goals, therefore must be adjusted accordingly, because it is unfair to evaluate students on content that they have not been taught. Granted, the process is far from complete; questions about specific facts still appear on many tests. Yet those changes are occurring, along with new methods of evaluation, such as portfolios and performance-based testing, which fit nicely with a curriculum in which students choose the content. The end result is that the curricular goals can now be met comfortably, no matter who chooses the content.

Less Time Spent on Behavior Management

Many teachers find it hard to imagine students beginning their classwork without being told, staying on task without being cautioned, and eagerly volunteering to do independent work. Those who have experienced such professional pleasures know that motivation cannot be forced upon students. It has to come from within. With traditional curricular models, students are figuratively dragged to the trough of learning. Their misbehaviors reflect their lack of interest in school content. For many, it is far more entertaining to derail the learning process.

When students choose what to study, misbehavior is reduced. Students are not being forced to learn. They are independent learners who have chosen their goals. There is no need for them to prevent learning from taking place because doing so will delay the process of finding out what they want to know. This process creates an atmosphere in which time on task is maximized, thus permitting sufficient time to reach the official goals.

Other Curricular Goals

Student Autonomy and Interest

In a series of classroom interviews conducted by Maria Yon, one of my university colleagues, my students indicated a preference for a class in which they chose the topics. They said that they valued not only the sense of power but also the educational implications. One student explained the benefits.

> Because then it's not just the teacher deciding. The kids get to say what they're going to learn. They'll probably be more interested in it, so they'll be more focused on it than if the teacher picked something that no one else was interested in. If they're interested in it, they'll learn more and the teacher won't have such a hard time.

The students deliberately chose controversial topics of personal relevance (e.g., abortion, gangs, guns) because, as one put it, "We'd never get that stuff in our other classes." Throughout the semester, and in interviews, the students frequently complained that they did not find the standard course of study particularly relevant or motivating.

Depth

Because the decision to change topics was student based, the students studied each issue until they were satisfied and ready to move on. This approach promoted more depth than the traditional survey approach that allows little opportunity for extended discussion.

Frequently, students asked questions that led to additional activities, which promoted depth of understanding. During their study of gang violence, for instance, some of the female students expressed interest in the violent activities of female gang members. The next day, I presented summaries of sociological studies on gangs that reported gang-imposed limitations on violence by female members. This finding evolved into a deeper discussion of gender differences regarding violence.

The choice of activities also added depth. When students examined state statutes on abortion, for instance, they complained that the lack of precise wording necessitated judicial interpretation. A simulation of the legislative process was then used to demonstrate how legislative compromise and negotiation often results in imprecise wording. This 2-day activity that had the students playing the parts of legislators, committee chairs, and lobbyists allowed students to experience the legislative process in a manner that is rarely allowed under the time constraints of traditional programs.

In the summative evaluations that were conducted at the end of each unit, the students demonstrated their depth of understanding. These essay exams required them to apply their knowledge, rather than recall a series of facts. The average grade on exams ranged from 80% to 90%.

In interviews, students commented on the in-depth approach, in contrast to the shallow-coverage orientation of their other classes. One student, for instance, who struggled for a way to describe his thoughts, preferred being "more centralized on one subject (rather) than skipping around a lot." In view of the students' profound interest in the subject matter, it is not surprising to find them enjoying in-depth study. This finding fits Dewey's (1964b) conception of students exercising their thinking skills when the subject matter is of their choosing. As most scholars will attest, thinking is an uncommonly enjoyable activity.

Summary and Cautions

Summary

Analysis of the data indicates that student curricular choices reflected their personal struggles and interests (e.g., violence, sexism, justice), with concerns ranging from the classroom to the overall society. The investigations into those topics had depth, with substantial discussion and analysis. Furthermore, the topics they chose to study fit the prescribed social studies curriculum. These results contradict the notion that students are not able to make responsible choices. It may even be argued that the choices made were more relevant than those in the mandated social studies curriculum. As predicted by Dewey (1964b), motivation and interest were not problems.

Class Size

The average class is much larger than the 12-15 students in the current issues course, but class size was not a factor in the curriculum development process. All important decisions were made at the whole-class level. In a larger class, the list of brainstormed topics probably would have been longer, small-group discussions would have been louder, and it possibly could have taken longer to reach a consensus. However, the way students choose content should not be affected by class size.

According to the research, class size does influence instructional methods (Passe, 1995). A large class makes it more difficult to manage several small groups or provide individual attention. Thus teachers of larger classes are more likely to use whole-group instruction. In the current issues course, about one third to one half of each class session was spent in small groups.

The use of small groups, however, is not required or even encouraged by the student curricular decision-making model. The choice of instructional activities remains with the teacher, who exercises his or her professional judgment concerning methods that will promote learning. My course could have included more whole-group work, but I prefer small-group activities because they help students develop their skills in cooperation, interpersonal communication, peer tutoring, and multicultural awareness. Although these benefits are important for all students, including adults, they are crucial for middle school students, because of their developmental needs (George & Alexander, 1993).

Teacher Role

The role of the teacher in this process should not be underestimated. Although students had considerable power over the curricular choices, my own knowledge, experience, philosophy, and skill made significant contributions. First, I had enough knowledge of social studies to move comfortably from topic to topic at very short notice. Second, my experience with the social studies curriculum and skill in managing a student-centered, process-oriented approach was instrumental in promoting depth and interaction. Third, my commitment to a student-centered curriculum and emphasis on process determined the types of activities that so engaged the students.

The process of meeting the state curricular goals for social studies was more subtle than it may appear. I tried to promote depth of understanding, but it was not with a conscious effort toward meeting any particular state goals. I had never examined the actual curricular document concerning middle grades social studies. It was only during the preparation for a paper that the substantial correlation between the course and the state goals was discovered. I was, however, quite familiar with the aims of social studies in general and may have used that knowledge when planning instructional activities. Teachers can maximize their curricular effectiveness by carefully aligning content with state and district goals. This process should take place through all phases of the planning process.

The key to successful planning is time management at the beginning of units. Time was not the major factor, however, in my ability to plan. As soon as the students' choice of topics became clear, I was calling potential sources of information and searching for resources in several libraries. A flexible schedule makes this process easier. If additional planning time is made available to teachers at the beginning of units, teacher stress can be reduced and the quality of instruction enhanced.

The Challenge

Although students' sense of autonomy was not specifically meas-ured, results indicate that students did enjoy having some power over the curriculum. That they used that power to contribute to a mean-ingful curriculum that met state goals in depth indicates that the process can work. Our challenge is creating the circumstances to make it happen.

6

Questions and Answers About Student Curricular Decision Making

An Interdisciplinary Curriculum

As a result of my experiences with student curricular decision making, I have given several presentations and workshops that describe the process. The educators and parents who have attended these sessions tend to ask certain insightful questions. In this chapter, I respond to the most common questions, as well as a few that may come up in your own efforts to implement the model.

Q: *Is it true that a curriculum that is chosen by the students tends to be interdisciplinary?*

A: Yes, because disciplines tend to be somewhat arbitrary in their boundaries. Science and social studies, for example, are forever crossing into each other's territory. Any discussion of such science content as energy, the food chain, and technology will inevitably lead to public policy debates concerning nuclear power, endangered species, and unemployment, respectively. These debates are traditionally found in the social studies classroom.

Consider other examples: Success in solving mathematical "word problems" is linked, in part, to students' ability to read and interpret the written word. The artistry of a ballet dancer or actor is developed through skills taught in physical education. The connections are endless.

When students choose what to study, they are unlikely to confine their choices to a particular discipline. They identify topics of interest that are almost always cross-disciplinary (see Figure 6.1). Life itself is an interdisciplinary concept.

Q: *How does the model's emphasis on interdisciplinary studies affect the organization of schools?*

A: It depends on the situation. For elementary school teachers, who tend to have self-contained programs, it is relatively easy to switch or combine school subjects. Students may never even notice when a study of spider webs evolves into a class poem on the subject or when multiplication is applied in the measurement of a map scale (see Figure 6.1).

Most elementary schools have specialists, however, usually in music and physical education, but occasionally in art, technology, and other areas. Quite a few elementary schools use departmentalization in certain grades. In those circumstances, as in middle and high schools, some form of joint planning is recommended.

Joint Planning and Teaching

Q: *Is joint planning feasible, considering the pressures teachers are under?*

A: Although the idea of an additional planning meeting appears to chew up the already limited planning time that teachers have, it actually can save time and promote learning. A lot of classroom content is repeated in different subjects. A science class on the circulatory system will present much of the same information on cardiovascular exercise (i.e., the heart as a muscle, how blood carries oxygen, effects of exercise on one's heart rate, etc.) as a physical education class. Research methods in language arts, social studies, and science frequently will overlap. The topic of Renaissance artists will appear in both art and history classes. Joint planning will save curricular time by eliminating redundancy. It will pro-

Many teachers have separate units on nutrition and the metric system. Those topics are unconnected in traditional school life because one deals with science and health and the other deals with mathematics. Yet children's basic experience with metric measurement comes from the sides of cereal boxes on which nutritional information is provided in grams. The savvy teacher treats both topics together, using the children's curiosity about the nutritional value of their cereals to get across some points about the sometimes mundane topic of metrics. Students benefit from applying their knowledge of metrics to nutrition, thus promoting depth of understanding (Passe, 1995, p. 281).

Figure 6.1. Dealing With Disciplinary Overlaps

mote depth of understanding by having students apply what they have learned in a variety of ways.

Joint planning also reinforces teachers' strengths and deemphasizes their weaknesses. Teachers who lack knowledge of a topic may benefit from planning with other educators. The geography teacher who knows little about geology could fill in the gaps resulting from inadequate undergraduate preparation by consulting a science teacher. Elementary teachers, who are asked to teach several school subjects based on a handful of undergraduate courses, are particularly hard-pressed to keep their knowledge base accurate and current. Many music, art, and physical education specialists would welcome the opportunity to integrate their subjects with classroom teachers, especially knowing that the units are based on student interests. Several other benefits have been found over the years (George & Alexander, 1993).

Joint planning is advantageous, but joint teaching is also beneficial. Specialists have a hard enough time getting to know and manage their hundreds of students. The added presence of the classroom teacher while their specialty is being integrated makes it easier to meet the unique needs of a class and the individuals in it. Behavior management is also more effective when two adults are present and communicating with one another. Finally, joint teaching creates opportunities to learn new techniques and philosophies, thus promoting professional growth.

Q: *Joint planning and teaching may be fine for elementary schools that are mostly self-contained, but what about middle and high schools?*

A: Many middle and high schools are ripe for restructuring. But you do not have to make a wholesale change. Those teachers who are interested in joint planning can do so on a small scale. Many teachers already have begun to do so. There are several reports of combined social studies and English courses, music and art specialists integrating their programs with core courses, and other combinations of teachers who seek to work together. Integration and team planning are basic components of the middle-school model. George and Alexander (1993) cite several examples of exemplary joint planning procedures and units in their classic middle school textbook.

Q: *It sounds great, as long as colleagues are willing to work together. What should be done about faculty members who are opposed to student curricular decision making or joint planning and teaching?*

A: These ideas are not for everyone. Many teachers will not support the model or are more comfortable relying on traditional curricular approaches. Some may see it as too complex or too time-consuming. Perhaps they believe that it will not work for their particular students. The program will not be successful unless the teachers are committed to it.

Within every faculty, however, there will be one or two potential allies who think alike on curricular issues. Those teachers may begin the movement, develop a program on a small scale, then fine-tune it before presenting it to the rest of the faculty. At that time, other colleagues may choose to join the effort. "Change is a process, not an event," according to Fullan (1991, p. 49).

Q: *Teachers who implement the model by themselves may teach some content that is assigned to another course or teacher. Is that a problem?*

A: It has always been a problem. It is not unusual for students to come to class already knowing all or part of the required content. Students learn a lot of school content outside the school building—from their parents, from the media, in church, and from hobbies, recreational reading, and other experiences. There is also substantial redundancy within the school at every grade level. Joint planning and pretesting are beneficial for any model.

When topics are student driven, the students are likely to learn the content more efficiently. If they go to the next class able to apply what they have learned from the previous class, it will probably make the new teacher's job easier.

Specific Subject Concerns

Q: *Why are there so few language arts topics on the various lists and webs?*

A: The lack of specific references to language arts merely reflects the nature of that subject area. Language arts are primarily skill oriented rather than content oriented.

Advocates of whole language recommend that language experiences be offered in context. Children read to find answers to their questions, write what they learn, constantly speak and listen to one another in the course of learning, and present findings to classmates when appropriate. Poetry, novels, drama, and other literature are available on every possible topic (Passe, 1995).

In the whole-language classroom, writing is integrated throughout the curriculum. Students do not write for the sake of writing. Instead, they use writing to respond to content in a variety of contexts (Passe, 1995). Chapter 4 describes how the middle school students wrote personal journal entries reacting to the case studies, research plans for their projects, directions to play their board games, and creative stories, scripts, and editorial cartoons.

Q: *Knowing that most students will not choose topics related to mathematics, how will those skills be taught?*

A: Every topic is related to mathematics! The topics listed in Chapter 4 all have mathematical connections. Students constantly were analyzing graphs and statistics, calculating averages, and estimating economic effects. They used measurement and geometry skills in developing their projects and interpreting and creating maps.

As with language-arts skills, mathematics content that is not tied to a real-life application tends to be ineffective. As a result of traditional approaches, many Americans suffer from a form of mathematical illiteracy that Paulos (1990) calls "innumeracy." They are constantly fooled by the numerical claims of merchants, advertisers, politicians, and even nutritional labels.

To counter this problem, the National Council of Teachers of Mathematics (NCTM 1989) has issued new standards to guide the mathematics curriculum (see Figure 6.2). The guidelines have four basic cornerstones, each of which is relevant to a curriculum revolving around student interests.

Q: *What about mathematics for elementary school students, for whom statistics are too complex and confusing?*

A: Suppose a first-grade class chose to study the school building. They could add the number of students in each class to determine the total school enrollment, calculate the difference between each class's size and the maximum allowed by the fire code, compare room sizes using various units of measurement, display the differences using bar graphs, and count the assortment of shapes in the architectural design. Instead of performing a mindless series of arithmetic drills, these children will be using their mathematical skills to solve problems. The math goals will be met, but in a more satisfying way.

Q: *Don't the students need a foundation in social studies and science before addressing issues?*

A: The assumption behind this model is that the basics are learned *when they are needed*. Otherwise, instruction is a chore, and students legitimately wonder, "Why do I need to learn this stuff?" The name and location of every African nation, capital, mountain, and river is not necessary as a prerequisite to the study of that continent. Students will learn about South Africa's geographic features when that information becomes relevant to the nation's current situation. The same is true for science content. The function of the liver will be best understood as part of a study of alcoholism, not as a topic by itself.

1. *Mathematics as problem solving*—formulating and solving problems, not just mathematical ones, and developing confidence in the ability to use mathematics meaningfully

2. *Mathematics as communication*—communicating in various modes, not just with numbers, to understand and get meaning from mathematics

3. *Mathematics as reasoning*—using both inductive and deductive approaches involving investigation, forming and testing conjectures, making and evaluating logical arguments, validating one's own thinking, and appreciating mathematics' contribution to sense-making

4. *Mathematical connections*—appreciating the integrated whole of mathematics, as well as the connections with other areas of human thought and activity (NCTM, 1989)

Figure 6.2. The Four Cornerstones of the NCTM Standards

Social studies and science are unpopular subjects because much of their curriculum is taught out of context. Such classic yawners as "How a Bill Becomes a Law" and "Chemical Compounds" become very exciting when presented in conjunction with units on "Abortion Laws" and "Pollution," respectively. Responding to student content choices allows for prerequisite knowledge to be learned as it is needed.

Q: *Are you suggesting that skills in art, music, and physical education also can be taught under this model?*

A: The leading teacher organizations in those areas have recommended integrated curricular approaches. The National Art Education Association has endorsed a discipline-based arts education model that integrates the arts (including music) across the curriculum (Getty Center for Arts Education, 1985). The developmental model of physical education, regarded as the most widely endorsed of several curricular models in the field, works toward the "total development of the individual socially, emotionally, intellectually, and physically" (Steinhardt, 1992, p. 967). These recommendations encourage joint planning and teaching.

Content Gaps

Q: *Isn't it possible that some required content will not be addressed during the school year?*

A: As discussed elsewhere in the book, that is already the case. With our ever-expanding required curriculum it is impossible to teach all of the required content and teach it well. As a result, graduates usually have substantial gaps in a variety of areas.

Keeping that in mind, the answer to the question is yes. It is definitely possible to leave something out. An entire school year may indeed go by without reference to Elizabethan England, for example. But that topic surely will appear sometime over the child's 13 years in school, perhaps in relation to one of Shakespeare's immortal quotations, references to characters like Romeo and Juliet, or in conjunction with discussions of Queen Elizabeth II. If a topic is truly valuable, it has to become relevant at some point.

Several topics may never turn up. The division of fractions is one topic that has little relevance, except as an exercise in logic. (Cutting a recipe in half involves multiplying by 1/2, not dividing.) Other topics, such as state flowers, the many uses of flax, and measuring the area of a rhombus have cluttered the curriculum for years. If they do not turn up in 13 years of school, how important can they be? We have enough useful content to teach without devoting time to unnecessary topics.

Q: *What happens if a question on one of those untaught topics appears on the end-of-the-year test?*

A: In the unlikely event that such obscure topics survive the test development process, most students probably would answer those questions incorrectly. But even if that content is taught, the students still might get it wrong. Knowledge and skills that we regard as irrelevant tend to be quickly forgotten. (Quick! Name five states and their flowers, three uses of flax, and the formula for the area of a rhombus.) It is when facts are learned in context that they are likely to be remembered. We may, for instance, recall that the orange blossom is Florida's state flower because we learned that fact in conjunction with the study of that state's citrus industry.

If end-of-the-year tests include such trivial content, the test developers should be fired! High-stake tests, including most college entrance exams, are based on broad curricular goals that put more emphasis on process than on specific knowledge. As discussed in Chapter 5, state objectives are becoming increasingly general. Coupled with the movement toward portfolios and other types of alternate assessment, the fear of overlooking minor topics should be of little concern. Besides, the depth and quality of student learning from a self-chosen curriculum should substantially improve test scores.

Applications Beyond K-12 Education

Q: *Can this model be used in preschools?*

A: Preschool children have always had a hand in choosing curriculum. No matter what content their teachers choose, young children are likely to steer the discussion toward the topics that interest them most. A gardening activity can easily become a study of ants when an anthill is uncovered. A storybook about a lion may evolve into a comparison of zoo experiences. A cooking experience may turn into a lesson on kitchen safety. This trend is not only true in preschools but also in Boy Scout and Girl Scout activities, family discussions, and conversations between friends. Indeed, it seems to happen everywhere but traditional classrooms.

Q: *What happens when college and university students make curricular choices?*

A: In many cases, they already do. Students are likely to choose electives that relate to their fields of interest. Teacher-education majors often register for electives in child psychology, nursing majors take counseling courses, and history majors select specialized courses on their favorite historical periods.

Within courses, it is quite common for postsecondary students to choose topics of interest for term papers and class projects. The choices they make are likely to reflect their needs. Thus, in a political science course, prelaw majors may choose to study Supreme Court cases, whereas business majors will focus on the issue of governmental regulations on corporations.

When I taught an Introduction to Education course a few years ago, I let the students decide what aspects of the field they wished to explore. To my great pleasure, they chose the very topics that were outlined in the original course proposals. Giving them curricular power gave them a feeling of autonomy, which translated into heightened enthusiasm for the course activities.

Q: *Is the model applicable to inservice education?*

A: Once again, that approach is already popular. School districts frequently offer a variety of inservice opportunities for teachers to select. Teachers who need help with classroom management register for workshops on that topic, whereas those who seek instructional improvement take other courses. Anyone who ever sat through a workshop on a topic of little or no personal interest will recognize the waste of time, money, and energy that comes with inflexible curricular mandates.

Curricular decision making works for preschoolers, university students, teachers, and other professionals. Learning takes place when children make curricular choices outside the school, such as with scouting, athletic teams, and clubs. Why shouldn't it work for students inside the school building? It does, as long as teachers are committed to using children's choices to promote maximum learning opportunities.

The Role of Teachers

Q: *Why bother having teachers if the students are making the curricular decisions?*

A: This model requires teachers who have curricular knowledge, instructional prowess, and management skills. To implement this model successfully, teachers have to be facilitators. This role entails recognizing connections between topics and content areas in order to prepare activities, as well as designing learning experiences that will maximize depth of understanding while incorporating thinking skills and affective goals. Teachers also must be able to constantly organize and reorganize students with differing needs while maintaining behavior standards. It is a challenging, but extremely rewarding, job.

Q: *How do I know if I can manage such a complex challenge?*

A: Many teachers would like to develop a student-based curriculum but are hesitant to do so. Starting off with a single student-centered unit is a good way to ease into the process. A middle school or high school teacher might try it with a single section before expanding the program. Elementary teachers may try it for a period of time each day, perhaps in the afternoon. At the end of the trial period, teachers should assess their own enjoyment of the process, in addition to student motivation, achievement, level of misbehavior, and the other factors discussed in the previous chapter.

Elementary teachers, who usually have self-contained classrooms, probably will find it easier to manage the program than teachers who meet with several groups a day. Teachers who have departmental schedules would therefore benefit from a gradual transition to student curricular decision making. As they and their students become comfortable with the approach, they will develop routines that will make the planning and instructional systems run smoothly.

Q: *Are there enough teachers who have been trained to lead classes in which students choose content?*

A: Several teachers already have programs in which the curriculum is flexible and students have a great deal of autonomy. It may not require a great leap to formally install a student curricular decision-making model. Whatever training deficits teachers have could be addressed on the job or through inservice.

Teachers of the gifted frequently design their programs around student needs and interests. They can provide significant input from their experiences by serving as leaders or mentors in a student-based curriculum model.

With the growth of magnet schools, a progressive administrator may be able to attract teachers who are interested in creating a special school or program within a school that is designed to give students curricular power. With several teachers working together—team teaching and comparing notes—the faculty members could, in essence, be training themselves and one another. Eventually, the body of professional knowledge they develop could be used to train teachers who are new to the school or program.

Quite a few public school teachers have left the profession or have moved to private, alternative, or home schooling situations because of dissatisfaction with the traditional curriculum. Some may be attracted back to the public schools by the opportunity to develop a student-centered curriculum. They can bring substantial knowledge and experience to a program.

A search for former teachers with an interest in and experience with student-centered education probably will lead to the local college or university. Many of the curriculum leaders cited throughout this book are involved in teacher-training programs. Most education professors would be delighted to work with teachers trying to implement a student-centered model. They would also welcome the opportunity to use student-centered classrooms and schools as teacher-training sites for their own students. After all, one of the problems in training teachers to use student-selected content is the absence of suitable models. The need for research on this model may also encourage professors to get involved.

Q: *Why would a teacher want to teach in a program that allows students to choose the content?*

A: *Teachers want to be effective.* Allowing students to make curricular decisions will promote an atmosphere in which students are motivated to learn content and skills. This will translate into academic achievement.

Teachers want to relate well to their students. Having to cram unwelcome knowledge down children's throats does not lead to positive teacher-student relationships. Serving as a facilitator establishes the kind of mentor role that many teachers crave.

Teachers want to teach. Too many effective instructors have quit because excessive amounts of class time are spent on discipline problems that are linked to student boredom. Additional time is devoted to motivating students to learn content that is not interesting or valuable. These problems can be reduced by giving students curricular power.

Teachers want to make a difference. They want to develop caring, autonomous citizens whose informed judgments will guide our democratic system. That cannot happen if students never have to make significant decisions. Teaching content that is irrelevant to the present and the future also reduces teachers' long-term efficacy.

Teachers want to be appreciated (and rewarded). Under this model, parents will marvel at their children's seriousness of purpose and dedication to learning. Citizens will recognize teachers who are motivating children to take responsibility for their lives. Political and financial support will grow when school is no longer regarded as merely a necessary hurdle to cross before entering the workforce. Relevance is a powerful tool.

Teachers want to use their skills. A college degree is not necessary if teaching merely requires passing out ditto sheets and reading aloud from the textbook. All of the courses in philosophy, curriculum, instructional design, and methods will be used, however, when teachers are managing a dynamic student-selected curriculum.

Teachers want to be stimulated. Student-chosen topics tend to be relevant and provocative. Teachers will find themselves intellectually engaged as they research their units. During planning and instruction, they will confront their professional beliefs and practices. When content is relevant to students, each class will be challenged by a variety of perspectives and a healthy dose of passion. Under those circumstances, teachers will actually look forward to the school day.

Q: *Is student curricular decision making a panacea for all that ails education?*

A: No. This model is not for everybody. It is unlikely to ever replace traditional curricular approaches on a large-scale basis. After all, many teachers, administrators, students, and parents would not be comfortable with student curricular power. But the model may help in reducing student dropout rates, keeping good teachers in the profession, and preparing effective citizens. Those are worthy goals!

References

Apple, M. W. (1982). *Cultural and economic reproduction in education.* London: Routledge & Kegan Paul.

Apple, M. W. (1983). Curricular form and the logic of technical control. In M. W. Apple & L. Weis (Eds.), *Ideology and practice in schooling* (pp. 143-165). New York: Cambridge University Press.

Boomer, G. (1982). *Negotiating the curriculum.* Sydney, Australia: Ashton Scholastics.

Britton, J. (1972). *Writing to learn and learning to write.* Urbana, IL: National Council of Teachers of English.

Caine, R., & Caine, G. (1991). *Making connections: Teaching and the human brain.* Alexandria, VA: Association for Supervision and Curriculum Development.

Deci, E. L. (1992). The relation of interest to the motivation of behavior. In K. A. Renninger, S. Hidi, & A. Krapp (Eds.), *The role of interest in learning and development* (pp. 43-70). Hillsdale, NJ: Lawrence Erlbaum.

Dewey, J. (1899). *The school and society.* Chicago: University of Chicago Press.

Dewey, J. (1913). *Interest and effort in education.* New York: Houghton Mifflin.

Dewey, J. (1936). The theory of the Chicago experiment. In K. C. Mayhew & A. C. Edwards, *The Dewey school: The laboratory school of the University of Chicago, 1896-1903* (pp. 3-27). New York: D. Appleton-Century.

Dewey, J. (1964a). Ethical principles in education. In R. D. Archambault (Ed.), *John Dewey on education: Selected writings* (pp. 108-139). Chicago: University of Chicago Press.

Dewey, J. (1964b). The child and the curriculum. In R. D. Archambault (Ed.), *John Dewey on education: Selected writings* (pp. 339-358). Chicago: University of Chicago Press.

Doyle, W. (1986). Classroom organization and management. In M. E. Wittrock (Ed.), *Handbook of research on teaching* (3rd ed., pp. 392-431). New York: Macmillan.

Fisher, C. D. (1978). The effects of personal control, competence, and intrinsic reward systems on intrinsic motivation. *Organizational Behavior and Human Performance, 21,* 273-288.

Fullan, M. (1991). *The new meaning of educational change* (2nd ed.). New York: Teachers College Press.

George, P. S., & Alexander, W. M. (1993). *The exemplary middle school* (2nd ed.). Orlando, FL: Harcourt, Brace, Jovanovich.

Getty Center for Arts Education (1985). *Beyond creating.* Los Angeles: Getty Trust.

Glasser, W. (1990). *The quality school.* New York: Harper & Row.

Goodlad, J. (1984). *A place called school.* New York: McGraw-Hill.

Goodlad, J. I., & Su, Z. (1992). Organization of the curriculum. In P. W. Jackson (Ed.), *Handbook of research on curriculum* (pp. 327-344). New York: Macmillan.

Grundy, S. (1986). *Curriculum: Product or praxis.* London: Falmer.

Kingston, R. D., & Anderson, D. H. (1982). A study to analyze curricular decision making in school districts. *Educational Leadership, 40,* 63-66.

Kliebard, H. (1986). *The struggle for the American curriculum 1893-1958.* Boston: Routledge & Kegan Paul.

Kohn, A. (1993). Choices for children: Why and how to let students decide. *Phi Delta Kappan, 75,* 8-20.

Knapp, M. (1995). *Teaching for meaning in high poverty classrooms.* New York: Teachers College Press.

McNeil, L. (1986). *Contradictions of control: School structure and school knowledge.* New York: Routledge & Kegan Paul.

Means, B., & Knapp, M. (1991). Introduction: Rethinking teaching for disadvantaged students. In B. Means, C. Chelemer, & M. Knapp (Eds.), *Teaching advanced skills to at-risk students* (pp. 1-26). San Francisco: Jossey-Bass.

National Council of Teachers of Mathematics. (1989). *Curriculum and evaluation standards for school mathematics.* Reston, VA: Author.

North Carolina Department of Public Instruction. (1985). *Teacher handbook: Social studies K-12.* Raleigh, NC: Author.

Passe, J. (1995). *Elementary school curriculum.* Madison, WI: Brown & Benchmark.

Paulos, J. A. (1990). *Innumeracy: Mathematical illiteracy and its consequences.* New York: Vintage.

Phillips, J. A., Jr., & Hawthorne, R. (1978). Political dimensions of curricular decision making. *Educational Leadership, 35,* 362-366.

Piaget, J. (1929). *The child's conception of the world.* London: Routledge & Kegan Paul.

Piaget, J. (1932). *The moral judgment of the child.* London: Kegan Paul.

Ripley, S. R. (1984). Student involvement in learning: An action theory analysis. Paper presented at the annual meeting of the Northern Rocky Mountain Educational Research Association. (ERIC Document Reproduction Service No. ED 254 527)

Shapiro, B. (1994). *What children bring to light: A constructivist perspective on children's learning in science.* New York: Teachers College Press.

Shor, I. (1992). *Empowering education.* Chicago: University of Chicago Press.

Steinhardt, M. A. (1992). Physical education. In P. W. Jackson (Ed.), *Handbook of research on curriculum* (pp. 964-994). New York: Macmillan.

Taba, H. (1962). *Curriculum development: Theory and practice.* New York: Harcourt, Brace, & World.

Tanner, D., & Tanner, L. (1975). *Curriculum development.* New York: Macmillan.

Vygotsky, L. (1962). *Thought and language.* Cambridge: MIT Press.

Yager, R. E. (1991). The constructivist learning model: Toward real reform in science education. *Science Teacher, 58*(6), 52-56.

Index

Activities:
  board game, 65-66, 85
  culminating, 49, 50, 61-63, 66-67
  current events, 47, 54, 67
  editorial cartoon, 67, 85
  introductory and review
    lessons, 73
  local application, 66
  planning, 43, 45
  student projects, 85
  synthesis, 47, 49, 63, 66
  videotaped dramatics, 61-63
Administrators:
  communicating with, 28-30, 41
  as constraints, 9, 32-33, 46, 94
  role of, during author's teaching
    experience, 54, 59, 60
  as supporters, 51, 92
Alexander, W. M., 79, 83, 84
Anderson, D. H., 12
Apple, M. W., 12, 26
Application, 4-6, 73, 74, 85, 86
Autonomy
  appeal of, for students, 76, 80, 90
  and emancipatory interest, 26
  goal of, 9, 13-14, 35, 92-93
  lack of, for students, 12
  and motivation 15, 19, 31

Behavior management, 17-18, 21,
  75-76, 83, 91
  boring tasks linked to, 17, 18
  self-discipline and, 18, 19, 48
Boomer, G., 26
Brain research, 19-21
  and cognitively demanding
    tasks, 23
  and complexity, 20, 21, 23
  and memory, 20, 21
  and searching for patterns, 20, 21
  and student experiences, 20, 23
Britton, J., 24

Caine, G., 19, 20, 21
Caine, R., 19, 20, 21
Constraints on student curricular
  decision making:
  administrators, 9, 32, 46, 94
  content coverage, 4, 68-78, 88
  controversy, 32, 41, 54, 59, 76
  end-of-the-year tests, 2, 3, 9, 75,
    88, 89
  parents, 9, 41, 46, 59, 60, 94
  planning time, 79
  political considerations, 30, 60, 93
  state and district guidelines, 2, 4,
    9, 12, 32, 45, 46, 68, 74, 79, 80, 89